A BRIDE PREPARED

FOR THE MASTER

A BRIDE PREPARED

FOR THE MASTER

by

MAURICE WYLIE

A BRIDE PREPARED
For the Master

Paperback ISBN: 978-0-95741-191-3
eBook ISBN: 978-0-95741-192-0

Published by
Maurice Wylie Media
Your Inspirational Christian Publisher

Publisher's Statement: *Throughout this book, the love for our God is such that whenever we refer to Him, we illustrate our honour to Him by capitalization of all references. On the other hand, we will violate the rules of grammar by withholding capitalization of all references to the devil, as we refuse to acknowledge him with any honour.*

For more information visit
www.MauriceWylieMedia.com

Contents

Acknowledgements

Because of their love, "A Bride Prepared" is in your hands.

To my first love the Lord Jesus Christ, without You this path in life would never have been walked. To the Holy Spirit who guided thoughts unto paper, sometimes I was unsure where the story was going and yet You have a way of making the impossible possible, allowing Yourself to become real through the ink of this book. To my Father in heaven, oh, how I love You, to have sent Your begotten Son for me, I can never repay, I can only jump into the freedom of Your love!

To the two men who brought the reality of God in my life.... My spiritual dad, John Hamilton and Alexander (Alec) Schofield, I could easily say as John the Baptist said, "The latchet of whose shoes I am not worthy to stoop down and unloose." Your testimony of our Lord and Saviour still lives on!

To my first lady, Maureen Wylie, "an uncommon seed" bringing forth an uncommon harvest of love and patience to the boy within me! You have helped release the man of God through me. Thank you for being my lady!

To the incredible team that God has brought around us locally and internationally to deliver our mission statement – 'Reach the maximum amount of people with a quality product to help change lives!'

To the saints are all over the world that stands with us, from the pulpits to the pew only one word could describe you – precious!

I thank you all.

Maurice Wylie

FOREWORD

"A Bride Prepared for the Master" is a must read for all serious believers in Jesus Christ.

The author uses Scripture, personal experiences, and colorful storytelling to convey strong spiritual truths needed by the Body of Christ in preparation for the return of Jesus Christ.

There are many books written about revival, soul winning, gifts of the Spirit, and many other topics but I truly believe "A Bride Prepared for the Master" contains quintessential insights needed before the Body of Christ can experience the end time harvest of souls and experience the glorious liberty of a latter rain glory awakening.

While reading you will be deeply inspired to allow the Spirit of God to open your eyes to any deceptive devices the enemy may be using to distract your heart from the true purposes of the Lord.

This book truly is a read for those wishing to be refined and made a "A Bride Prepared for the Master".

Apostle Demontae Edmonds

Freedom 4 the Nations (USA)
Covenant Connections Ministry Alliance

INTRODUCTION

There's probably nothing more romantic than a man asking a lady to marry him. The eyes of the lady light up as she responds with, "I will!" These words do not mean that she is married; they mean that she is promised, engaged, contracted, that she is single minded and has but one desire – to be 'faithful unto the end.'

But what about when the thrill of that romance wanes and a desire rises for another? Is it possible that a covert team from the evil one has sought out and found a weak area through which to launch a deadly attack? Might not that person be in a spiritual war, not having been prepared for it?

Gravity cannot be seen with the eye, only its effects, and the same is true of the spiritual world – we cannot see it, we can only see its effects.

Jesus proved this when He came out of the virgin's womb and walked this earth as the Son of God. He declared that another world exists, one more real than the world in which we live (John 8:23).

This brings us to a conclusion, which is, that around us is a spiritual world that seeks to make the invisible visible.

When the invisible world of the evil one gains an opening into a life, it smashes through any vow that was made and enters into every family and every bloodline, into the closest personal friendships, showing no mercy to those who surrender!

Like a knife piercing a heart, it separates that which was faithful, that which was true, that which said, "Faithful to the end!" The most precious relationship no longer means anything. But where did it go wrong? How did this happen? Where did the problem begin?

Viewed naturally, we might think it was during that first kiss, that first sexual act, or when the secret relationship came to light. But what if it was not that kiss or that first sexual act that caused us to abandon what we deemed true and best for us? What if something far more sinister was in play?

From the physical act of adultery to its spiritual counterpart, we will expose its very root. Both inside and outside the Church this Adulterous Spirit is rife, seeking to break the covenant we made with our marriage partner and with our Groom, Jesus Christ. If we are to be truly free from this spirit, we need to understand how it works, so that when the "King of kings" returns, His Bride the Church will be free and will have but one thing on her mind; her faithfulness to the Groom.

As you journey with me on this road of discovery, you will laugh, cry and maybe even get angry. But do not fear; emotions are there to let us know that we are alive. The stories you will read are real, the names and characters have been changed only to keep private the identities of those involved. As you read you will soon grasp that you are not the first one to have gone down this path; and you won't be the last. But I pray that as you see the Light, you will know that someone is waiting to set you free. His name is Jesus, and He can take that which the devil planned and turn it around for your good.

Remember that it's not over until the final whistle blows. I invite you to become "A Bride Prepared!"

Under His Shadow.

Maurice Wylie

Chapter 1

The Hunter Within

There she was: a beautiful young virgin, still in her teens and with the greater part of her life still ahead of her. She was still speaking the language of the young, and was innocent in both mind and body. Little did she know that the day was fast approaching in which her life would be changed forever.

The young girl was being eyed from a distance. Thoughts of how nice she would be had already seduced the mind of the Hunter. A plan was needed. How could the hunter set the trap and what could he use for bait?

Like any predator, the Hunter sought to get as close to the prey as possible before striking the life-changing blow. He noticed that every morning she walked the same path and spoke courteously to those she encountered along the way. He saw that her manners were second to none.

One morning, while watching the girl leave her home, the Hunter decided to move closer, so as to be on the path along which she would walk. He would pretend not to notice her approaching. His heart began to beat faster as he sensed that her presence was close. When she was within a few feet from him, he turned and faced her, smiling as he said, "Good morning!" She responded with a quick smile and words that brought him comfort. "Good morning to you!" As she walked on, his burning desire surged, nearly overwhelming him, and as he looked her up and down his mind went wild.

That night the Hunter tossed and turned in his bed. Her lovely face, her cheerful voice, her fine figure – these were constantly in his mind. It seemed that no matter what he did or what he tried to think about, one thought and one thought only was on his mind – she would become his prey!

He could not wait any longer. Early the next morning he rose and for what he deemed to be his first date, showered and put on his body those things that would make it smell nice. Looking in the mirror, the thought came to him that he would be an exceptional gift for this girl.

While impatiently waiting for the time of her appearance, images of what he would do and how good it would be flooded his mind. Sweat began to soak his collar. The time had come to walk the path again.

Over a period of days the Hunter had timed the walk and had found what he reckoned would be the ideal place to spring the trap. The question was: would the prey fall for it?

Here she comes, he thought, right on schedule, speaking to each person she meets, enjoying the day that is unfolding before her but not for long!

She approached the place where the Hunter was in hiding and suddenly he pounced. Startled but remembering that she had spoken to him only the day before, she said, "Hello!" This brought the previous day's greeting to mind, and he replied, "Good morning!" But this time was different. Suddenly he grabbed her! In shock, she thought that what was happening was unreal. But by the time she realised what was happening the Hunter had swept her away. The trap had worked. It had snapped shut. And the Hunter had his prey.

Chapter 2

The Lady in Waiting

She was raised in the house of the Lord by parents devoted to godly principles, her father teaching her the ways of God and her mother the ways of motherhood. The latter prepared her to be the best wife she could be. She held these precious mother-daughter chats close to her heart. These quiet talks would happen suddenly when, out of nowhere, their hearts would open and they would begin to share intimate things. Her mother was preparing her for the day when she would stand as a Lady in Waiting.

From the outside, her family was normal enough. Her brothers would quarrel with her and she would respond. But although they teased one another, woe betide the person who came against any one of them – for such an act united them instantly!

She had some idea of what she would like to do after she finished school. She would get a job that might become a career, and when Mr Right came by she would marry him and they would continue their lives together, living out their dreams.

This particular day started out just like any other day. Her father prayed with her and as usual gave her a big smile and a hug, the kind a loving father reserves for a much-loved daughter. His strong arms enclosed her securely, melting away any fear she had for the day ahead. Then she ran over to her mother and throwing her arms around her, nearly squeezed the life out of her. Her heart was singing as she left the house and began walking down the path.

Like every other morning she met the same people. "Hello, how are you?" was the most familiar greeting. With a spring in her step, she was thinking of how everything in life was going so well for her. She could not help but smile from ear to ear. Making her way down the path, she suddenly heard a voice she was familiar with say, "Good morning!" "Hello!" she replied, and as she did his hand, the hand of the Hunter, clamped her mouth closed, and lifting her small frame from the ground he carried her off.

Paralysed with fear, she was unable to scream as he threw her to the ground. Her mind was in shock. What is going on? Is this really happening? Where are all the people I know?

Then, suddenly, energy seemed to come from nowhere, and she fought hard to beat him off; but her strength was in vain against the hunger of the Hunter.

Time seem to stand still as she was raped and acts of gross indecency were forced upon her. Like a lion roaring in victory over its prey, the Hunter's chest swelled, for he had achieved what he had set out to do: steal the sweet innocence of the Lady in Waiting. She knew that she would never forget what had happened to her. But how could she tell her family?

When he rose from her, grinning, the Lady in Waiting struggled to get off the ground and onto her feet, while trying to cover herself as best she could with the clothing that had not been torn from her. The hair that had shone earlier that morning was now messed up and dirty. The skip that had been in her step was now gone. Not only was her body shattered but her life as well! How would she tell those she loved what had happened?

When she approached the door of her home she could hear her mum singing one of her favourite songs. Tears welled up from deep within as in her mind she felt that she had let her parents down. Quietly opening the door she edged through the doorway into her home. She did not know why she still felt vulnerable as the door closed behind her.

Her mother came out from the room opposite, and seeing her little girl's face, her mother-heart caused her to lunge across the hallway, so that her arms could embrace her little girl. Tears streamed down both faces as they fell to the floor holding each other. Nothing could ever be done to remove the memory of the foul act that had taken place.

Minutes passed as the mother nursed her little baby. What that mother wouldn't give to remove the pain from her child! Gently, she persuaded her to tell what had happened.

Then the question that cut the mother's heart even deeper. She asked what any mother would ask. "Do you know who did it?" While waiting on her daughter's reply, men's faces flashed in the mother's mind. Was it this person, was it that one? Or was it someone unknown to her?

Understandably, her daughter found it hard to speak. Was it that she didn't know him, the mother wondered, or was it that she knew him but was too scared to tell? The mother kept coaching her until the words came out, "Amnon, my brother, did this!"

The words were like a sword thrust into her mother's heart, and she doubled up with the pain of what she had heard. That her daughter been raped was bad enough, but that the rapist was a son was almost unbearable. Incest was found in the house! Nothing could be worse!

You may be thinking that all this is just awful. In fact, you might even be asking if this is a true story. What if I were to tell you that this story is in the Bible? You would be shocked! But what I like about the Bible is that it's about everyday life, and for this reason it holds every answer about life that you will ever ask. For me, the Bible is not just a book of information but a book of instruction, one that brings revelation. We should not read it just to gain information, for knowledge will only puff us up. Instead we should seek instruction through the revelation it imparts, which will cause us to grow up.

The basis of this story is Second Samuel, Chapter 13, and yes, I have brought the story into our time. The Lady in Waiting is Tamar, from the family of King David. The story is true, and what happened to Tamar has been repeated to this day, both inside and outside the Church.

Are you the Hunter or the Lady in Waiting? Perhaps you are neither. But know that this still happens within families, including God's family, which we will go into later. These days, the Hunter can be either male or female, as can the person in waiting.

When I refer to a man or a woman, in most instances this is interchangeable. As important as it is to know that not all men are bad, it is equally important to know that not all women are good. Tamar was an innocent young woman whose half-brother couldn't live without taking her innocence, and because of this foul act he would later be killed.

On the pathway of life there is a Hunter who is seeking after prey, and for the Hunter to be stopped, God must be permitted to step in and reveal the path of deception and destruction.

Get ready, as we go into "The Garden of Adultery" and unfold to you where unfaithfulness began.

Chapter 3

The Garden of Adultery

Adultery is not a new thing. How old is it, you may ask, and when did it first happen? Adultery first took place at the very beginning of time. "That far back?" you may ask. Yes, the devil has no new tricks up his sleeve, just old tricks presented in a new way.

Always remember that you will not be the first or the last to suffer, and you need to know that there is a way of escape. But to understand the escape plan, you must understand the situation in which you find yourself.

Way back at the beginning of time, God made Adam, and then brought to him a wife and put them both into a garden. The two then became one flesh (Genesis 2:21-25).

Can you imagine what life was like for Adam before Eve was formed? As a single guy, he had authority over everything. He had control of the animals and the beautiful garden paradise in which he lived. Most importantly, he had a wonderful relationship with God; so much so that they talked together!

God had decided that the man needed to be a giver, and for him to be a giver he needed someone he could give to, someone who would appreciate his gifts; someone who would be very much like him.

The time came when God decided to perform the first ever operation on man. While Adam slept, God removed one of his ribs, and from it formed a woman – man with a womb.

I'm sure that when Adam awoke he felt a bit peculiar; as though something was missing; but after careful examination of his body he could see no difference.

After doing his usual rounds in the garden, Adam laid down for his siesta, and as he dozed he could sense something closing in on him. Slowly opening his eyes, he saw a beautiful person who looked like him yet was somehow different. His mouth fell open and he smiled from ear to ear. A wife had been brought to him! This would be a day to remember! From the moment they met, Adam and Eve thought only of enjoying the rest of their lives together.

Love was in the air! He loved her and she loved him. We might say that when God made Eve from Adam it was a match made in heaven.

Like all good things, Adam and Eve's marriage was wonderful, and days slowly passed into weeks, and weeks into years. But a day was coming when a third party would cause them to look outside of themselves; the Adulterous Spirit was about to enter the garden.

When God brought the woman to the man, they had everything in common. They did everything together. Their love for each other was unquestionable. The two were one in every way.

However, a day came when one of the two that had been become one flesh thought as an individual, and when this happened it gave room for a third party to enter, in the form of a serpent; and you know what they say in relationships three's a crowd.

The third party came into the relationship dressed in something that enticed, that seduced, that said, "I can give you more than what you have!" At that precise moment, adultery waited for the opportune time when the two that had stood together as one were divided.

The woman, drawn into the conversation with the third party, began to commune with the serpent.

In my years of ministry, I have heard many times that what happened was the fault of Eve; that if only she hadn't communed with the devil everything would have been different. But let's look more closely into this story, so that we can put what took place into perspective

Genesis 2 v 19: *"And out of the ground God formed every beast of the field and every fowl of the air, and brought them unto Adam to see what he would call them: and whatsoever Adam called every living creature that was the name thereof."*

God brought every kind of animal to Adam. They all came to him and he named them.

Something I find interesting here is that all the animals were brought before Adam for him to name (their name described their character), but in a moment of time the devil slipped through, meaning that Adam must have relaxed his authority, and in so doing a serpent came through the hedge and bit him (Ecclesiastes 10:8).

Adam was told to **'hedge'** (Gen 2:15). This is an old King James word used to explain what farmers then did. They would walk around the field boundaries and check to see if a hole had been created in the surrounding hedge. If they found a hole in the hedge they would "hedge it", take branches and close the hole in order to stop animals from getting in or out of the field.

As you read the Scriptures, you will learn that at some point Adam became complacent. For when the devil, disguised as a serpent, spoke to Eve, Adam should have spotted that something was out of place. But no, he was content to stand near her. Genesis 3 v 6 "*...and she took of the fruit thereof, and did eat, <u>and gave also unto her husband with her</u>; and he did eat.*" Please note Adam stood close enough to be with her but not close enough to separate her from the temptation. The third party came in and the spirit of adultery did its evil work.

Could it be that you are in a garden, as Adam and Eve were, and are listening to the voice of a third party?

Who is the third party? It can be anyone who leads you outside your partner or your relationship with God. It can be the hand that holds you and tells you that you're not alone, the touch on the shoulder that says, "Well done!" It could be the smile and the sparkle in the eye that reveals interest. Or it can be an idol of some kind that causes you to live a life of spiritual adultery, instead of a life of faithfulness between you and God. When you are being led outside of God's will for your life, you are surrendering to this spirit.

It seeks to cross the hidden line, a line that it was never meant to cross, but is so often allowed to. This third party will lead you down the road of destruction, and will destroy what you have by promising that which you may never ever get. The plan of the third party is based in deception. Let's uncover it!

Chapter 4

When Normal was Abnormal

The Secret Place

I have never met someone who does not have a secret they are careful to hide. I grew up in deception, and even though one may not seek deception as a lifestyle, that which you are born into and raised up with is what you eventually become. For me, secrecy was a lifestyle, and it was only when I encountered the reality of God that I realized how flawed my character was. So much of what I thought was normal was in fact abnormal.

Before we go any further, let me ask you a question. Do you know that God has secrets? But what difference is there between the secrets that God has and the secrets you and I have? God's secrets have one thing in mind – the goal of them is nothing but good. God's Word says in 1 Corinthians 2:8:

"But the rulers of this world have not understood it; if they had, they would not have crucified our glorious Lord."

Why did God keep the secret of what Christ's crucifixion would mean from the devil? So that you and I could be fully purchased with the Blood of the Lamb for our sins! Now that is what I call a good secret! The secrets of God are like jewels that are there to be seen by those with eyes to see them, unlike our secrets, which are hidden very deep, because we would be so ashamed if someone were to expose them!

I love finding out God's secrets, and these are only found when we operate under the revelation of the Word of God, for when we do that we are discovering that which has not been revealed; "the secrets of God!"

In the world of secrets, we create a few lies to cover our tracks. "White lie" statements expand the truth, but in reality by telling them we are really lying. You see, a "white lie" that covers a secret is a deception, and where there is deception there is a secret hidden in the heart that no one is allowed to discover. Without your permission *not even* the Holy Spirit can get into this hidden place. It's your comfort and your security. Should something not work out you can return to it. It's what we might call PRIVATE or MINE! And this place can hold many secrets.

To unravel the Adulterous Spirit you must realise that it cloaks itself in deception – layers of it, one deception after another – deception that covers its tracks, so that in time it can manifest its plan of destruction for your life.

What may at the start be deemed as innocence can lead to the destruction of life, family, ministry or whatever. We need to uncover the secret place if we desire to walk in the Light of God, which is our calling.

For me, deception started when I was very young. There were times when people would come into our home and I would be told to leave the room. "It's not for your little ears," I would be told. You knew something was not right, even as a child, when the next day you heard someone ask, "Had you any visitors last night?" The look your elders gave you brought fear, and you knew the answer was going to have to be "No." At a young age I was being introduced to a world of dark secrets, one based in deception that had its roots in fear!

In our minds we fool ourselves that the secret place is one that even Jesus cannot find. How deceived we can be, and how deceived I was!

There I was having just surrendered my life afresh to God, and yet trap doors hid covered places that still remained, places that I could not remove.

Sometimes in life things happen that made such an impact on us that we are never the same. When I was young, somehow or other a group of us boys and girls, some of them in their teens, all got together and what can I say? The innocence of childhood fought and struggled against what was happening to me. What was supposed to be a little bit of fun and daring became an addiction in my life.

As I grew older, other guys saw me as someone on the road to life. I was searching like a predator, taking the spoil, and then moving on. I thought this was normal. But God had other plans.

Even after I surrendered my life to Christ, I still had the addiction and how I struggled! It was like Dr Jekyll and Mr Hyde. I was thirsting for more of God, and yet every so often this lust would rise from within and seek gratification. Many a time I cried myself to sleep. How could this be? I was saved but in many ways it seemed I was still lost! The battle began like a tennis match. I would hit the ball and lust would hit the ball back. And just when I thought I was winning, the ball would go out of play and I would fall yet again.

When I look back, I now realise that it was only after my life was surrendered that this fight really began in me. A war was going on, and sometimes in those dark times, being honest, I was unsure if I would come out on the winning side – such was the ferocity that waged.

I remember driving through the town where I lived, and seeing a woman walking along the road. Without even trying to think, in my mind I could see her naked. I kept thinking that there had to be a way to find peace of mind. Every day this would happen, as floods of filth invaded my mind. Many a night I slept with the Bible under my pillow, thinking that perhaps it might help.

Then one day things changed. I saw a woman walk pass, and as usual, automatically she was undressed before me. But this time a prayer came out of me for that woman – "Father, I ask that you would save that woman, baptize her in the Holy Spirit, lead her to the place where she will cast out demons and heal the sick!" It was as though an elastic band broke over my head – Snap! Something happened inside my head, and for the first time I felt that I was able to be free. From that moment on, God turned around for good what the devil had planned for evil. When the devil drew my attention to a woman for a bad purpose, I would react by praying for her. God gave me a key that turned the fight around in days, and the devil stopped producing the images of women I had seen, because he knew that whatever he would bring into my mind I would bring forward for prayer.

God can turn around the evil the devil has intended for you.

The Bible says, "*What you sow is what you reap*!" (Galatians 6:7) Have we ever considered what we do or say in front of our children, sows seeds into their little lives? One of the greatest teachers in this area is my wife Maureen. The number of times she sacrificed her feelings and emotions for her children knocked me over, as we would say in Ireland. Her love for them was manifested in her protection of them.

This was the very opposite of how I grew up. All I ever knew was family turmoil. I was moved from pillar to post. Those who were in my life one day were gone the next. I say to those of you who have not experienced this lifestyle that I am so happy for you! And for those who have sought to find an identity, I understand the turmoil that you have been through or are going through.

From childhood to adulthood, seeds are being sown continually. Unintentionally or not, words such as, "You're useless, you'll come to nothing" can plant seeds which can take root in our life.

Like weeds continually appearing in a nice garden, the only way to get rid of them is to pull them out by the roots. But this is beyond the ability of small children.

I'm all too aware that some things can be passed down. It's like handing a child a heavy weight and telling them to walk straight. That's impossible, because no matter how hard the child tries to do so, they will buckle under the weight. Perhaps, as it was in my case, a weight borne by your forefathers was handed down to you, and no matter how hard you try to straighten yourself, you grow into adulthood with a character that is deformed and you don't know it. The Bible calls this iniquity – a weight that is handed down to you from the spirit world; and as you yield to the iniquity, you become that which has been handed down to you.

This iniquity is the opposite to the Anointing of God, for it also has strength and power, but does not even sit equal to the Anointing of God, which is true and good for you. Iniquity is of the devil, is built on deception, and is bad for you. It comes with a built in self-destruction button and can destroy you and those around you. Deception seeks to capture you and turn you into someone else.

God's anointing seeks to lead you to places and people that will add blessing to your life. The iniquity of the devil leads you to places and people that will remove blessing from your life.

The iniquity I had in a particular area caused things to happen so easily that I didn't even have to try. The right person would come across my path, things would happen, and I would move on. However, the

Anointing of God creates divine appointments and opens up doors like you would not believe!

Bondage is like being in the hand of a great puppeteer. From childhood, circumstances would cause an impact on the mind and in turn would deform the character. How can this path of destruction be brought to an end?

Shortly after I came back to the Lord, I was invited to attend a meeting in which a man called John Hamilton was speaking. It was a house meeting in the countryside. That night we packed the car with people and drove off to a farmhouse in a rural area.

Little did I know that on this night I would experience things that would change my life forever!

We arrived at the house about an hour before the meeting was due to begin, and it was full of people who were all very excited. The meeting started with some singing, and after a while, John Hamilton was introduced.

The warmth of God's love that oozed from him was so overwhelming that I was drawn in irresistibly. I could hardly prevent myself from staring at him.

He began to share his testimony, and as he did, I felt a love for God in him that I had never before witnessed.

Before going any further, I have to let you into a secret, and I suppose there's no better place than "The Secret Place" to tell you about it. I was in a relationship with a girl for several years, and knowing what had happened to me as a child I'm sure you will not be surprised when I tell you that not all things were pure between us. Some things are hard to give up; especially when you enjoy them.

That night the lyrics of the song I was singing penetrated my heart.

"Go through with God, thy vows do pay
Thy life upon the altar lay
And the Holy Ghost would do the rest
He'll bring to you God's very best!"

I am no singer. In fact if you heard me you may want to leave the room. But that night those words brought me to an altar of self-sacrifice, and I knew that God was calling me to lay my life down completely. In my spirit I knew the price - that doing so would cost me my flesh. But to this day I still would pay the price for the One that I love!

As John ministered by sharing his testimony, it was as though no one else was in that room but me. Even though I was seated in the back row, I felt that I was in the frontline, being shot at with invisible bullets that never seemed to miss. I remember that each time he would look down in my direction, I would smile, and "Amen" would come out of my mouth. Religious or what? Isn't it amazing how we can put on such an act?

When the meeting came to an end and the last 'Amen' had been said, I took off like a rocket toward the exit! Close proximity to this man who allowed God to shine through him was all too much for me. I had grown up learning to protect myself and to keep people at a distance, either for my safety or theirs. My sprint to the door seemed to be working, and yet somehow or other as I was going through the door a hand gripped my arm, and to my amazement it was John! He said to me, "God has shown me things about your life! I want to see you privately before you go home!" "No problem," I responded, "I will come back in!" Little did John know (or did he?) that this boy was not about to go back in, this boy was going home, and in a rush at that! For the first time in my life I was scared of facing the unknown.

You see, I was raised in a part of Northern Ireland known as "the murder triangle", an area in which murder and bombing was all part of daily life. I had shaken the hands of death many times without flinching. Darkness had been my shelter for many years. But this, this was something new; this was genuine love, love such as I had never before known and I was scared of it.

Looking back I know that it was fear that drove me through the door that night and out into the car, while shouting at everyone, "Get in, I'm in a rush to get home!" But the people I had brought with me wouldn't get in the car. Worse still, I didn't know my way home from this isolated farm house. Talk about being stuck between a rock and a hard place! And to make it even worse, I wish I could say that the love they had for me was why they wouldn't get in the car; but no, they were just being nosey. They wanted to hear what this man was going to say to me!

So there was nothing for it but to go back in and face the unknown. I felt like a mouse being thrown to a cat that hadn't been fed for days. Would I come out alive? That was my concern.

As I entered the room John was talking to some people, but when he saw me he excused himself and walked straight to me and said, "Please follow me!" I followed him like a lamb to the slaughter, and as we entered a room he closed the door behind him.

John grabbed my arms with his hands and those tiny eyes of his looked up into my eyes and he started to cry, saying, "God has shown me things about your life!" You know, I said to myself, "Aye, right!" (As in, I don't believe it.) But John just kept on revealing secrets that only I knew – and it was blowing me out of the water!

You see, if you and I together did something secretly and some person called me into a room and began to tell me about it, then I would come to the conclusion that you must have told him. This was different, because secret after secret was being told to me by John, and I knew that no one else could have known them. Not only did he tell me what I had done in my past in fine detail but was also able to tell me what I wore at the time, the colour of the clothes, and so on!

Dark impossible secrets were exposed and something inside of me snapped. From my innermost being a cry of pain rose from deep within me. It was as though someone who had been forced to do things suddenly found out that he would never have to do them again. It was deep cleansing of the pain that sin had afflicted me with. God's blood was washing the shame of my past away. I had struggled to keep things I felt ashamed of away from God, but God's love came and overwhelmed me that night. Yes, after what I experienced that night, I still walk like Jacob with a limp in the flesh. I will never be the same again. That night "The Secret Place" was uncovered by a prophet, and I pray that as you read on, the secrets that separate you to any degree from the One who loves you will be uncovered, and that His manifold presence will take hold of you like never before.

Chapter 5

When the Needle Sticks

If you have passed a certain milestone year of your life, you may remember the vinyl record player. Had you been one of those people who owned a vinyl record player, you may have come across its weakness, which, like any other weakness, if not sorted leads to trouble.

As a young teen I would often take a loan of my mum's record player to listen to the latest music of the day. It was while I was listening to a song that it would happen. The player's weakness was that its needle would stick at a certain place on the record, causing me to hear the same word, again, again, again, or the same line again, again and again. The record was playing, the music was playing, the voice was singing, but in fact none of them were going anywhere!

This is what happens to us when we only understand half a truth. We think that we are going somewhere, but in reality we are going nowhere. Like the record player, we are stuck in the same place, repeating the same thing over and over again. Let me share a true story...

The phone rang and my wife was informed that a child of God had been sent to a mental institution. When we hear that such a thing has happened, a righteous anger rises in us – how dare the devil do this to one of God's children!

Paula had sat under the teaching known as 'name it and claim it' for several years, and had been taught that if you confess it, confess it, confess it, you shall have it.

Because the lady did not receive the fullness of the revelation she confessed to the degree that it took her mind over the edge and for her own sake was admitted to the mental institution.

When my wife and I went to visit Paula, she was being monitored twenty-four hours a day. To our amazement, when we came into the room where Paula was, all we could hear was: "I have the mind of Christ, I have the mind of Christ, I have the mind of Christ!" Sadly, whilst she walked the floor continually repeating over and over those same words, her face showed only that of a tormented soul.

This may be stepping on some toes, but I would rather squash toes than miss an insight. I simply cannot accept that someone has the mind of Christ and yet needs to be placed in a lock-up unit for their own safety; no matter how much they maintain that they have the mind of Christ. Could it be possible that in this case the teaching she received caused her to step out of Faith into Hope, while mistaking it for faith? But, you might ask, what is the difference between hope and faith?

Hope is like a lady longing for a man to ask her to marry him. It might happen but then again it might not. You hope that your team is going to win the match, but that's not always the way it turns out. Hope, like the team you follow, has with it a degree of uncertainty!

Faith is entirely different, for it is not based on us but on God. As Hebrews 11:1 says "Faith is". Not will be, or has been, but is! Faith is in the present. Faith *is*!

We can hope that God will heal, but faith declares that God has already healed us, for faith *is*!

You may have heard the following verse quoted, "*Faith comes by hearing and hearing from the word of God.*" (Romans 10:17) There is a BIG difference between hearing a word from God and receiving mere knowledge of the Bible.

What is the difference? Jesus was the Word made flesh (John 1:14), but was not born to merely give a message. He was born upon this earth because He *was* the message. Jesus never quoted Scripture for the sake of Scripture or taught it just for the sake of teaching it. He, being made the manifestation of the Word, revealed the right Word at the right time to the right people at the right place. He came to align himself to their understanding. What happened to Paula was that she had been taught knowledge, which in itself is not wrong, but knowledge without understanding is not just wrong but damaging.

Think of it as teaching a four year old the square root of a number, when they don't even understood that one and one makes two. It's not that the square root is wrong, just that the teacher would not have grasped the learning level of the child. As it is in the natural, so it is in the spirit. Leaders: let's not use our platform to demonstrate how much knowledge we have, but rather let us use our ministry to sense where the people are at spiritually, and take them forward a step at a time. If we do this, then the promised land that is their right to inherit will be their destiny.

Peter, disciple of Jesus was one day sitting in a boat with the rest of the disciples. Knowing men, I would say they were very likely talking men's chat. But something in Peter made him look round and then leave their company. Curiosity drew Peter towards the side of the boat, leaving the rest of the disciples looking at each other. They may have said, "He never finishes a conversation." Or, "Have we offended him?" Or, "Where is he going now?" But Peter, even though known for putting his feet into things without thinking, is like many of us! Within us a kind of spiritual radar searches out things. Is Jesus doing something we have not yet seen; is He moving somewhere we have not yet been?

While the disciples were still wondering what Peter was doing, they heard Peter shouting "Can I come?" The Lord's response was wonderful. He was coming towards the boat walking on the water and responded, "Come!" Up until that point, no matter how much Peter would have confessed, no matter how much Scripture he would have quoted, he would have sunk into the water, if he had stepped off the boat. The key to faith is hearing God's voice and then doing! When Jesus said "Come!" an invisible path of faith was laid before him and true faith always takes you closer to Jesus.

I like what Reinhard Bonnke said, "Peter never walked on water he walked on the Word that Jesus gave!" Faith is not hearing a teaching - faith is hearing from God and obeying. Like the record player sticking and repeating the same word again and again Paula was hoping, hoping that she had the mind of Christ. Hoping that whatever she quoted would come to pass. However, hope without understanding put her into a mental institution until a day came when she realised where she was at in God and built on that and in doing so we are glad to say that she is now out of the mental hospital and rebuilding her life.

The question is – Are we in hope? Hoping for a relationship which is not right under God to become right as we continue to confess and believe? Or are we in faith where no matter what has happened we live our life based on the standard of God's Word, what God says we will do, where He says we will go – Faith is hearing the voice of God and obeying!

Chapter 6

CUT ME IF YOU CARE

While my wife and I were visiting Paula in the mental institution, another woman, who we shall call Heather, made friends with us. Over several visits, Heather told us that she had been in the mental hospital for more than six years, most of that time in the lock-up ward.

A day came when we sat with tears in our eyes as she told of the time when she played an instrument in her church, and how she loved playing it to God. Sadly however, when she had a nervous breakdown her minister came once and never returned.

As we continued to befriend Heather, she began to trust us, and one day she felt so free being with us that she came into the waiting room wearing a T-shirt and a pair of shorts. You might be thinking: What's wrong with that? Previous to this she would always have worn slacks and a long sleeved shirt, but now she felt free to reveal her real self. I suppose in some way she may have been wondering, would we still love her?

I saw in that moment something I had never witnessed: every inch of her arms and legs had been scarred from being sliced and burned. Heather was a self-abuser.

Why would one who was so beautiful inflict pain by cutting herself and doing herself such damage?

As I sat there, one part of me – the religious side said, "How dare she do this to herself!" The other part of me said, "I could cry after seeing so many cuts and so much self-harm on a body!" While I was thinking on these things and trying to come to terms with them in my little mind, my wife ran over to her and threw her arms around her and held her tight! When she did, Heather broke into tears! For the first time someone still loved her; even after seeing the scars of her self-abuse.

You see, Heather was expecting my wife and I to walk away like everybody else had done. For us to do that would have inflicted more cuts to her heart but in her reasoning we would have cut her heart with our actions in the way she had cut herself with broken glass and cigarette burns. We decided under God that we would stand by her until there would be a breakthrough for her. Her mind might have been saying, "Cut me if you wish" but her heart was crying, "Don't let go of me, no matter what you see!" If you're like me, you would be asking what must have happened that someone would abuse herself so much.

We learned that as a young child Heather watched as her father walked out of her home and never came back. She never saw him again. Loneliness brought questions. Was she to blame? These unanswered questions bounced and echoed into her future. Sent regularly to Sunday school and church, she learnt to quote the Bible. Her talent for the trumpet led her into the worship team of the church, and each Sunday she would play her heart out to God. Somehow she had started to come to terms with her life. Maybe it hadn't been her fault that her father had walked out. Maybe life now was beginning to get better!

One day, while her mum was out of the house, her uncle called to visit. But this day would be different. Her uncle had become aware of the approach of her teen years, and when he left that day he had taken something from her that would make her feel dirty for many years. Heather was back to where she started, "Was it my fault this happened? I feel so dirty so helpless!" Her mum never understood why overnight this nice girl fell into fits of temper and rage. Her trumpet unblown, Heather now had a secret that haunted her.

The brightness of her school days had just dulled when she began to ask herself: "Why should I care to live when terrible things happen in my life?" To escape further pain she decided to take her life. Opening the kitchen drawer she selected the sharpest knife, and slowly but surely drove it into her wrists, pulling it from left to right. Then, falling to the ground in a faint, she lay there in pools of her own blood.

Heather awoke to find herself in hospital. Her mother had returned to find her lying in her own blood. Social Services, a government body that helps those who are in any form of trouble, had been notified, and were now to enter her life.

For days, weeks and months she was monitored, until they believed that she had outgrown that season of her life. By the time she was eighteen she was back at church, only this time she was playing the drums, which she enjoyed. Then she moved into her own apartment, thinking that maybe she could forget the terrible things of the past.

At the end of her teenage years, she happened to be out for a stroll in the local park. Unfortunately, she was so enjoying the walk she didn't notice that the park, with its lovely trees and scrubs, was empty of people. Night was falling. Sad to say another type of night was to enclose Heather. She was attacked and raped within a hundred yards of the security of her home. This put her mind over the edge, and she went from the hospitalization of her body for the damage that had been done to it, to the hospitalization of her mind – locked up in a mental institution for a number of years and under the constant administration of drugs. And even within the secured wing of the mental institution, Heather would still find ways of self-harming.

Each visit required us to go through a number of security doors. This unit was located in the furthest part of the hospital grounds. It was as though there was no other human existence. The sound of the large metal doors locking behind us as we went through from floor to floor was an experience in itself. It was no place for the faint hearted. Witnessing those tormented souls throwing themselves to the ground, some squealing, others ripping out their hair with their bare hands, made me wonder more than ever: Where is the Church of Jesus Christ? Did Jesus not come to set these people free? It was at that point – the time when we first met Heather, when my wife and I decided that just because one church had let her down there was no reason why others should let her down.

During the months we visited Heather, her consultant began to see changes. Instead of swallowing broken glass, she began to show signs that she wanted to live. Slowly but surely, and for the first time in six years, Heather was going in the right direction.

Transferred from the lock-up, where at all times she had been escorted by six staff members, Heather was moved to a non-secure wing of the hospital. It was approaching Christmas, and my wife sensed that God would let her out over Christmas to visit her family. It would be the first time in six years that she would see Christmas outside. The church we attended at that time had been prayerfully faithful in supporting us, and I shared with our pastor what God had laid on my wife's heart regarding fasting and praying for Heather. Our pastor had taken it before God and a forty day fast was put in action, with a rota made out so that every minute until the end of the fortieth day was covered in prayer.

The 23rd December arrived, the day the fast ended, and our home phone rang. Heather was on the line. She said to my wife, "You'll never guess! The top consultant has just signed the order for me to be released for three days to be with my family over Christmas!" Oh, the overwhelming joy we shared at this wonderful news was something that words are just not enough to explain. We give God all the glory, honour and praise for the love and freedom that Heather was now about to experience in her life.

"Cut me if you Care" is all about a person that maybe was not unlike you or someone you know. OK, you might not be slicing yourself with a knife or broken glass, but what you are doing is cutting across the principles of God. The result is that you are harming yourself!

Pain can be a wonderful thing for self-abusers, because the pain within is so great that inflicting pain outwardly distracts from the pain within.

For some, the pain of hearing news that one can't bear can lead them to slam the door of their life and head off into a life of adultery. Why? It's because pain has been inflicted on them, and the infliction by them of further pain distracts them from the main pain. But, as we have learnt, this is just self-deception.

Hurt causes hurt. Disappointment follows disappointment. Our external hurts reveal our internal hurts. We may make excuses for our actions, but if the seed of Christ is within us, then Calvary has wiped away any excuse we can have. Let's learn how to clean the slate of such excuses.

Let me tell you about "The Chicken Factory."

Chapter 7

The Chicken Factory

Have you seen the film "Chicken Run?" There is a BIG difference between that film and actually being a chick in the 'Chicken Factory?'

The real 'Chicken Factory' is normally based on a conveyor belt system – it's all about speed and keeping that chick going from one end of the factory to the other. The chicken arrives in one form and leaves in another form entirely; and the less hassle to the operator the more profit.

Could you be that little chick on a conveyor belt in 'The Chicken Factory'? That little chick caught and put onto a conveyor belt system without even knowing where it will take you?

It's Sunday, the belt is moving, and off you go to church. You say hello to someone, raise your hands, clap in the right places, listen to someone preach for thirty minutes (or maybe an hour), and then sing again. Oh, and let us not forget the drawn out offering, during which you are made to realise that you are only blessed when you give money.

But the "Spirit that raised Christ from the dead dwells in you" and stirs you to look for a way to get off the conveyor belt. Oh, I am not talking about leaving the Church, but about leaving the system. You may have been told that to ask or move out of the conveyor system is rebellion, which is like witchcraft, and no-one serving God wants that so like an obedient chicken you go back into the middle of the belt and let it carry you through the process.

One day on this belt you get a glance at how it ended for others who began just like you, and ask, "Could that be me?" The chicken is barely recognisable; its bones are just about all that is left, and the meat it once carried has all been chopped off! The conveyor belt system has taken its toll. Somehow or other a spark shoots through your heart, igniting in you the thought that this could be your last chance to escape 'The

Chicken Factory.' You look around to see if there is anyone else like you, but your eyes can't see very far, and anyhow, all the chicks are all looking one way and are happy clucking, just as people do in their praise to their church, their pastor, and their worship team. But you now know there is more – you know that you have not been called to a predictable end but to a higher calling!

The years that you spent in the system adapted you to the few pieces of grain you were being fed each Sunday, and the head bird catcher told you to stand strong in the Lord! In realising that, maybe the picture that was painted when you first got on the conveyor belt was merely a distraction to keep you on the belt and to not ask questions. So you decide to take your chance by jumping off the conveyor belt.

When you flutter to get off only to find yourself falling, you have to place your faith in God rather than the system. This realisation is life-shaking! As you fall and the floor seems to rise to meet you, you know in this moment of truth that God is either real or He is not!

When the chicken is but an inch from hitting the floor, an arm reaches out and it finds itself secure in the palm of a hand. As the chick is gently lifted, the cry of its heart is: Please, please don't put me back on the conveyor belt; let me die! Better that than rather just exist! Another hand covers the chick's head, and with one hand under and one over, the chick cannot be seen – it is hidden in the hands of someone who loved it enough to save it. The movement of these hands is so gentle and so sweet that for the first time the chick falls into a sound sleep. No longer is it toiling in torment, no more is it striving to succeed. Sleep seems to stream out of every part of its body. Its years in 'The Chicken Factory' had taken their toll; it hadn't known just how much.

When the chick awoke, it breathed air that was fresh, and every breath brought a freshness of life. A plate of food had been placed in front of it, the right texture and amount of food that it required and for the first time strength began to return to its body.

As the chick became aware of its new surrounds, it watched other chicks doing things it had been told not to do.

There was something different about these chicks. A voice rang from within their hearts. It said, "That which I have put in your heart to do you can do!" With freedom in the midst and competition removed there was but one purpose – to be that which their Creator had called them to be: unique!

As Psalm 139:14 so well states, *'We are wonderfully made'*

If ever you are to leave "The Chicken Factory' you must first realise that you are totally unique. That there is no one before you and there will be no one after you that will ever be the same as you. Created in the image of God, you are unique!

Listen carefully – You are not called to be different, you *are* different! This may sound like a cliché but there is a BIG difference between believing that you are called to be different than being different.

If I constantly strive to be different then I actually believe that I am not unique, which cannot be true. If each tree leaf is different, then surely you and I are different in our own right. If you can grasp the revelation that when God created you, He placed in you a seed called uniqueness; you are not called to be Fred, Jane, Maurice or anybody else. You are called to be you. It is your uniqueness that God uses, and in finding that uniqueness you will also find your freedom to be YOU!

What I am sharing with you I learnt firsthand under the anointing. While ministering in a leaders' conference these words came out of me: "You are not called to be different; you are different!"

Your DNA is unmatchable. You do not need to be a copy or try to be a bishop, getting everything right, or waiting to be named Right Reverend. No, you just need to be you! For the first time those leaders saw themselves as leaders and not copies of other men. Know this and know it in your heart: no one else in the world is the same as you.

You might wonder what this has to do with adultery. Putting in front of you the image of another is idolatry, which is spiritual adultery. Seeking to be someone else and not the one the Master created is surely adultery to the Master! For when you're not you then you're someone else. But who made you into that image? Who allowed that? What happened to you that caused you who were born unique to be so much like so many others? Could it have been 'The Chicken Factory?'

In trying to be someone else you lose your identity, which was part of the reason why you were born. If you have allowed this to happen, it will allow weakness to come into your life.

We must take on the responsibility that Adam relinquished. We must learn to get rid of Mr Hyde!

Chapter 8

Becoming Someone who You are Not

If you remember the story of Dr Jekyll and Mr Hyde, it is about one man of two different characters. Both show themselves through him. One day he's Dr Jekyll, the good guy, and the next day he's Mr Hyde, the bad guy. How did Dr Jekyll become Mr Hyde? A chemical was injected into his bloodstream that caused a reaction, with the result that at different times he changes into another person. As Mr Hyde he does evil things, things that as Dr Jekyll he would never do. When he is Mr Hyde any evil thing can happen. Could it be that a Mr Hyde lives in us?

Mr Hyde operates out of the dark places, living a life of secrets ruled by fear and lust for satisfaction. When the Adulterous Spirit comes into your life, you become someone that God never designed – you become a Mr Hyde. You begin a life of secrecy, a life of lies and fantasy, a life that will lead to your destruction!

It may be a relationship that begins with a prayer partner or a work colleague or your next door neighbour. It may start in innocence over a cup of tea, a time of prayer, during a stay behind for work. It may start in innocence but can end with you being pronounced guilty.

It's the sparkle in the eye, the flutter in the heart, the spring in the step, these are all things that we must look for when we are in the company of another, for in the moment you sense that person's interest but are married to another, you are surrendering to the Adulterous Spirit.

Adultery is a thing the Church has accepted within its walls. Oh, you may think "How on earth can he say that?" Firstly, let me say that the Church of Jesus Christ is full of this Adulterous Spirit. It manifests itself at every corner. Why would I say that? Adultery happens when the third person enters a relationship. In the case of a marriage, this means an outsider, a third person. In the case of spiritual adultery, it means someone else coming between you and God. In either case, if you are a Christian, may I ask: "Is a third party involved in the relationship?"

When God first gave the Law He wrote it on tablets of stone. The commandments of that Law have been written in our conscience, so that we know what is right and what is wrong. In fact, most of the cultures in the world were established on these principles.

Let's pick out a couple regarding this "Adulterous Spirit!"

Exodus 20 v 3

"Thou shalt have no other gods before me."

The Webster Comprehensive Dictionary carries the following definition of the word 'God' and 'god'

God - The One Supreme Being, self-existent and eternal; the infinite creator, sustainer, and ruler of the universe, conceived of as omniscient, good and almighty.

god - A being regarded as possessing superhuman or supernatural qualities of powers, and made an object of worship or propitiation; a higher intelligence supposed to control the forces of good and evil; a personification of any of the forces of nature or of some human attribute, interest, or relation; a divinity; deity.

Any person or thing exalted as the chief good, or made an object of supreme devotion.

Anything that absorbs one's attentions or aspirations: Money is his god

When we read, "Thou shalt have no other gods before me this is relating to 'god' with a small 'g' as in the second group of the word's meanings.

How many of us would have a small 'g' in our lives, one that takes up our focus, our aspirations, our devotion to the point that some would call it worship?

This 'g' can be anything, including the church you attend. If the worship team, the minister, the building, the whatever, were to be removed - what then? Would you still be inspired? Would you still hunger for the Master; or would you need the small 'g' to comfort you? The desire of the small 'g' must be removed and replaced with only one thing - the true God. He alone is worthy of our devotion, our service, our dedication. It is for Him alone that we should live!

Another commandment we should look at is Exodus 20 v 14 *"Thou shalt not commit adultery."*

Adultery - Webster's Comprehensive Dictionary

1. The sexual intercourse of two persons either of whom is married to a third person, unchastely (enjoying impure thoughts and acts), unfaithfulness.

2. Any lewdness (lustfulness) or unchastely (enjoying impure thoughts and acts) of act or thought, in violation of the divine commandments.

Based on the understanding gained from Webster's Dictionary, adultery can be intercourse, which is what people normally deem it to be. However, if you are a Christian and read the Dictionary of Jesus, the definition would be more like the second. As Jesus would have put it, if you even think of these things you have committed adultery in your heart. (Matthew 5:28)

Based on these commandments and the words of Jesus, it is quite obvious that adultery begins when the mind wanders off on its own ways and finds another way.

When this happens we are committing adultery against God, because we have now lined ourselves up with a third party; and remember that I said, "Adultery is when the third party comes into play on that which two have been made one." We need to draw again from the strength within and refocus on the One who has called us. Samson was told, "You will have your strength as long as you do not cut your hair." (Judges 16). But Samson entered into a relationship and shared that which was intimate between God and himself with a third party. In so doing, he opened himself up to destruction. Let's start closing the door on the third party. Let's get back to God's original plan, which is or you and your partner as one in marriage; or as you and God as one, without another in between. Learn how to close the door on the third party and block the devil's path of destruction that he has for you. Are you ready?

Chapter 9

The Gooseberry

We have a word in Ireland for a third party involved with a couple who are dating – we call them a 'gooseberry'!

What is "a Gooseberry?" A Gooseberry is the third person between the two lovers. It is said to have originated back in the early 19th century with the practice of a chaperone keeping "herself busy" picking gooseberries, while the chaperoned couple had some time to themselves.

The Oxford English Dictionary confirms this use of "gooseberry-picker", so this explanation is quite convincing.

You know how chicken you were on your first date; you needed all the encouragement in the world. You may have asked a friend, "Please accompany me on the date!" Note - The third party has just been invited to get involved. If you didn't know this by now, please take it from me as good advice – sooner or later the 'gooseberry' needs left behind! "Two's company, three's a crowd"!

Likewise, in your spiritual or natural walk you must come to the point where anything that even smells like a 'gooseberry' must be cut off and left behind; that is, left behind in the past. There is no room in the future for 'gooseberries' – you must get rid of them!

This Adulterous Spirit is a 'gooseberry'. It is there as the third person, the 'hanger on', the one that clings on and does not want to let go.

Most of us do not like pain. But being in Christ we must be ruthless with this Adulterous Spirit, to the point where cutting it off becomes first and foremost. The pain that comes with cutting it off becomes the secondary issue.

You might be in a secret relationship now, one that brings with it false comforts. But sooner or later it will be exposed and when that happens, what was done in secret will be revealed openly.

My friend, I want to get to you before that ever happens. As in the story of Samson, there are people who are waiting for us to fall. Many will "boo" you when you're down, and very few will ever extend their hand to help you get back on your feet again. For them to do that would show that they were associated with you, and you and I know that most people who attend church don't like to dirty themselves with the problems of others, lest they themselves be accused of the same.

That's what I like about Jesus, He waded into whatever needed doing, standing up for the innocent, providing a get out clause that would show the way of escape for the guilty. Is it any wonder that the Bible says there is none like Him!

Although the Bible is deemed religious by the people who do not know it, for me, and hopefully for you, it is a Book of Life. Its pages give us insight into the fallen human race, and the revelation of a glorious God who loved His creation enough to reach out to it – and to continue reaching out to it even after we messed it up. If you are not yet into the Bible, I highly recommend that you get into it!

There is a story where the Adulterous Spirit is in play and Jesus is brought right into the middle of the situation.

Jesus is in the Temple and is teaching the people who have gathered there. During His teaching the masters of the Law come into the Temple, dragging behind them a woman, whom they then throw at His feet. Jesus, being the coolest person who ever lived, doesn't even move as all this unfolds before Him. The Scribes and the Pharisees say to Him, "*Master, this woman was taken in adultery, in the very act.*" (John 8 v 1:18)

You have to imagine these Scribes and Pharisees huddling round one other. They must have been peering through a hole or something to have seen the act while it was taking place. Are you aware that even the Scribes and the Pharisees were wrong in what they did? In the story of Noah (Gen. 9 v 22 – 25), his son Ham saw his nakedness, and because he exposed it to others he was cursed. These Scribes and Pharisees clearly state they had caught this woman in the act, which means they saw the woman's and man's nakedness, which itself brought them under judgement. But their willingness to see people as below themselves caused them to be blind to their own sin.

Have you ever asked what happened to the man who was with the woman? Did he not also do wrong?

Religious people half-quote Scripture so that acts that are done are not understood; and the storyline here makes no difference.

With these Scribes and Pharisees only taking a woman they had broken the Law. Let's read some Scriptures

Lev 20 v 10 *"And the man that committeth adultery with another's man's wife, even he that committeth adultery with his neighbour's wife, the adulterer and the adulteress shall surely be put to death."*

Deut 22 v 22 *"If a man be found lying with a woman married to a husband, then they shall both of them die, both the man that lay with the woman , and the woman: so shalt thou put away evil from Israel."*

Against their own doctrine, these religious people were involved in watching a sexual act take place, but contrary to their own doctrine they brought only one of the two persons involved in the adultery. Also, against their own customs, they interrupted the teacher.

Jesus, being not just a teacher of the Law but a manifestation of the Law, knew all these points and instead of bringing judgement on them all brought mercy and a way of escape from the situation they had brought about.

Jesus said to the woman, "Go and sin no more!" Her exposure to the Light (Jesus) brought her not only forgiveness but also freedom from the sinful situation.

To the Scribes and Pharisees Jesus said, "He that is without sin among you, let him cast the first stone at her!"

A common feature in Israel in those days was stoning a sinner to death. These people would have been involved in doing that because they had been witnesses to the act of adultery. For them to have not to have stoned this woman only says one thing – they realise that Jesus knew they too had broken the Law, and that they themselves were also guilty.

No matter what stage you are at under the influence of the Adulterous Spirit, as with the woman caught in the act of adultery, God has now brought you to the place where you know that Jesus is waiting on you. For many of you, religion has stood ready with stones on which were imprinted words such as condemned, isolated, ridiculed, rejected! They were ready and willing to throw them at you with all of their might. But the good news is Jesus stood in the way. Jesus never died on that Cross with His arms closed so He could not grab you. No, He held out His arms so He would never miss catching you.

You are within the sight of the greatest catcher in the world. Throw yourself at Him with confidence, for He has never missed a catch!

Are you ready to be caught?

Chapter 10

Catch Me if You Can

Desire is in the heart of each one of us from the moment of birth, and the things we desire most are love, acceptance and approval from those around us.

What happens though if we are not on top of the list when it comes to looks or personality? Well, for me starting a new school in the middle of a year was nerve wracking. My teachers, classmates and surroundings were all new to me. I was the new kid in school. On the second day the teacher said, "Outside for football!" I could hardly wait, I was so excited! I ran out with the others and lined up as requested, but then felt vulnerable, as though I was in front of a firing squad. The teacher called out two of the boys and said, "Each of you pick six pupils!" Standing there with excitement, wondering which team would I be on, my only thought was, "Hurry up and pick me!"

The names rang out of those they knew were best at the football. Stephen, Paul, John, Matt, James… On and on they called. But where was my name? Where was Maurice? The excitement within me began to drain away as those around me were called forward, but not me. Only two names were now left: George and mine. A tiny spark of expectancy flashed within me: am I about to be chosen? The answer was no. I felt as though a big bucket of water had been thrown over me, as George's name was called, and the teacher pointed to the other team and said, "You just go over and join that team." He didn't even know my name.

I don't remember whether or not I played well that day, but I do know that I was the last one chosen to play. The knowledge that I was not desired as a team member made a huge impact on me.

Before you start feeling sorry for me, let me tell you that my deep need to be desired drove me to compete hard in every football match, so that never again would I be picked last. I wish I could tell you that I became the number one choice, but in all humility I must confess that although I did rise somewhat in the ranks, it was never to the top. That position was for the real footballers.

Not long after a baby is born it just lies there and smiles up at you in a way that tells you it wants to be desired. Before long it begins to speak words that are not found in any English dictionary, and you copy them and speak them back to it. What are you doing? You are responding to the simple expressions of its desire to be loved!

Desire is a wonderful thing – The dictionary defines desire as: "An eagerness to obtain or enjoy; a request to obtain; to wish for the possession or enjoyment of." (The Graduate English Dictionary)

We would all agree that desire is a major part of a meaningful relationship. There are few things more satisfying than enjoying the company of the person you love, and obtaining their permission to further enjoy their company takes desire to a higher level.

We all have desire built into our nature. It may be the desire for a drink, for fries, for chocolate, for a new car, or for a date with someone of the opposite sex. Marketing companies spend heaps of money trying to find out what we desire, and after obtaining that information, do all that's in their power to place the thing we desire right there in front of us. Why? They know that through our desire they can clinch sales of their products and to them sales mean profits!

Have you ever asked yourself if desire is still as important a part in your relationship with your marriage partner or your relationship with God as it once was? If not, you are in a dangerous place, because desire is a natural part of your makeup, and if you have set aside the desire for your partner or for God, then you have unwittingly opened yourself up to a desire for another.

Desire rises from a need, a want, a longing that seeks to be filled. It passes its needs through an information highway in our brain to the point that we can see it and taste it, even though we do not yet have it. Desire can focus the unfocused, bring strength to the weak, and harness the vision.

"What if you have set desire aside?" Note that I did not ask, "What if you do not have desire?" You need to cement into your heart the fact that desire is an intrinsic part of you; it is how God made you. You were made to desire!

From a young age we seek affirmation, the pat on the back, the hug that says we're secure. This is part of our nature, designed and built into us by God.

You need to come to the point where you fully accept that God made it natural for you to desire and to be desired.

Scripture says in Proverbs 18:22, *"He that findeth a wife findeth a good thing..."*

The amount of times I have pondered over this verse, "He that findeth a wife findeth a good thing!" This verse of Scripture clearly states that if you find a wife you find a good thing; in other words it is good for you to find a wife – plain and simple!

However, if every wife in this world was a good wife, there would be no bad wives – and you and I know that this is not so; the odd bad wife is out there, I am sure!

We need to settle certain things in this life, and an extremely important thing that we need to settle (especially as Christians) is that the original text of the Bible is infallible.

Since the original text of the Bible is correct, and yet it is possible to get a bad wife, then the conclusion must be that we have misunderstood the text, which says, "If you find a wife you find a good thing."

If we are to understand this, we must dig a little deeper...

God made man male and female, in His own image (Genesis 1:27). But not all men are husbands and not all women are wives. Let me explain. In a marriage ceremony in the Western world, a man and a woman exchange rings, put them on, and say, "I do!" However, we have read, "He that findeth a wife..." Does that mean we need to find another man's wife? I don't think so!

An important fact we learn about Truth is that all truth is parallel. Even within the church system we put people into positions and called them Apostle, Prophet, Evangelist, Pastor, Teacher. If the truth be told, it is some man rather than God that put most of them in.

God creates the person for the office, not the office for the person. In other words, Mr Know it All is not made a pastor because his name is Know it All. That person was already an Apostle, Prophet, Evangelist, Pastor or Teacher before some man put him in that position. Let's look at this more clearly. In 1 Samuel, chapter 16, the prophet Samuel is instructed by God to go and anoint David to be king over Israel. David is away out in the sheep field minding his own business, singing away to himself and his sheep, when all of a sudden a servant comes running to him, saying, "The prophet Samuel is looking for you!"

You must realise that the prophets in Bible days were not at all like the ones that bring us nice, encouraging words for us to be sure that they are from God. If you believe that God does not correct through the prophet, you need to wake up! Samuel brought such a fear of the Lord wherever he went that the people trembled at his coming! Now I call that the kind of meeting you would not want to miss! Not only that but in this story David has just been told, "The prophet Samuel is looking for you!" God was waiting for David!

While I was ministering in a youth conference in Berlin, God revealed to me what I'm about to share with you. That night there was such a hunger for God in those young people that you just knew that God was going to meet them at their point of need.

I told them that David had six brothers whom father favoured more than him. Do you know how I know this? The six were called by the father for the position of king, but David was not. Have you been overlooked, as David was, while others were given chances? No doubt you remained faithful even after you were, but it's only natural that you would have wondered why them and not me?

Jesse, the father of the young men, lined them up, and Samuel walked towards the eldest son, the firstborn, to anoint him. The first born son was normally God's choice. As Samuel was about to anoint the oldest God said, "He is not the one!" Samuel moved on to number two, who also was rejected. The same thing happened again and again, right on down the line to the last, number six. Without doubt this must be the one, Samuel thought, but God said, "It is not him!" Imagine if you were in a situation like this; that God had instructed you to anoint someone's son, and the father lined up all of his sons, and that when you came to the last one,

God said to you, “This is not the one.” How many of us would panic, standing there with anointing oil and no one left to anoint? Some of us would quickly pour the oil over him and run, hoping that God didn't notice! But what I like about true prophets is that they just keep going regardless. Samuel asked Jesse, “Are all your sons here?” Jesse probably thought hard for a minute or two before answering, “Oh, could it be my youngest son David you're looking for?” Eager to deliver the anointed word from God, Samuel would not sit still until David came. David: the boy shepherd; his father's youngest son. It was then that God told Samuel, “Arise and anoint him, for he is the new king!”

According to tradition the eldest (first-born) should have been chosen, more so because he was a soldier, but God passed by the prophet's choice and instead chose David. But I want you to realise that this raises a very important point, which is that when God chose David, He also chose his family. If Samuel had anointed another of Jesse's sons rather than David, the entire family, David included, would have been lost. Remember that it was David who ran at Goliath, while his brothers, whom man would have chosen as king, ran the opposite way.

Why did God pick you? Before the beginning of time God had seen David's brothers running away in the heat of battle. Likewise, in you he saw someone who could believe for the impossible! God knew by anointing David He would save the entire family. And, just as God chose David to reach his family, He has chosen you for the same purpose!

At what point was David made king? Some would say that it was when Samuel anointed him. Others would say that it was when David took the throne years later. I would say the key to when he became king is found in 1 Samuel 16 v 1 “*...I have provided me a king among his sons.*” David was ordained by God to be king before his birth, and the anointing for kingship was to release the prophetic for the people to witness in 2nd Samuel 5 v 3-4. David was a king long before ever being crowned king openly – he just never realised it.

According to Jeremiah 1 v 5, the prophet did not become a prophet when he took his office, but was a prophet in his mother's womb. Through many examples, the Bible clearly states that those He has chosen do not become a title on the day that they stand up in front of people – they walk in that title/office long before man recognises it.

Now to return to our first Scripture: "He that finds a wife finds a good thing." Do you see that God is saying that the wife is already made, that everything is already within her to be that wife? God did not bring Eve to Adam for her to become a wife. Eve came as a wife to Adam, having been taken from him, in returning she added something to him. That is what a wife does – she adds.

Marrying a woman does not itself make her an ideal wife; it makes her a woman who now wears a ring. If you are in search of a wife or a husband, remember to look for one who has character before placing a ring on her finger! If you can learn the difference a lot of trouble may pass by your house.

To have a suitable wife is the most wonderful thing imaginable. In fact, such is the wonder of a wife that the Bible parallels the relationship of a husband and wife with that of Jesus the Bridegroom and "His Church".

Chapter 11

Dare to mention the L & L

For some of us it may take years to learn the difference between **L**ove and **L**ust. For me, I used to think Love and Lust was really the same thing spelled differently. If you lusted after someone you had love for them; that was the way I saw it.

To keep it simple, the difference between Love and Lust is Love gives and Lust takes. So right now I would remind you that this is why the Bible says God is love (1 John 4:16) and does not say that God is lust. There's a huge difference between the two words.

When God began to reveal to me the difference between Love and Lust, I realised that I lusted when I thought I loved. Lust is a beast that came into play in man after the Fall. But it was originally discovered in Lucifer when he lusted to be higher than God.

Isaiah 14

12*How art thou fallen from heaven, O Lucifer, son of the morning! How art thou cut down to the ground, which didst weaken the nations!*

13*For thou hast said in thine heart, I will ascend into heaven, and I will exalt my throne above the stars of God: I will sit also upon the mount of the congregation, in the sides of the north:*

14*I will ascend above the heights of the clouds; I will be like the most High.*

Lust can never be satisfied, because whether in the form of power, recognition, or sexual satisfaction, Lust is a task master. Lust will continually whip you, only for you to find out when you get that which you have lusted after, you still lust. How many bodies will be abused before we come to realise that the problem is we are trying to fill a bucket named Lust that has holes in it? When will we come to our senses and realise that a bucket that has holes in it cannot be filled?

Lust was the drive behind the Hunter, in the first chapter. Those of you who have a problem with lust very likely saw yourself in that chapter. You may be either male or female, lust knows no bounds. Oh, you may not have raped from a legal point of view. But honestly, how many of us saw a person as a target and went after that person as an objective. When that bull's eye was hit we just got up and walked away. In the words of the song it was a case of "Another one bites the dust!"

Lust's twin is Pride, and each feeds off the other. One demands satisfaction and the other thinks it deserves it. Where you see lust there is also pride; the two work hand in hand.

If you are already in adultery, lust has been the one who has driven you from your marriage partner into the arms of another. Note that I did not say the bed of another! Adultery is not just sex with another person. A court would define it as such, but Jesus defined it as intent. We may be citizens of the country in which we were born, but we belong to another country, another kingdom, one that has a higher set of laws!

As you can now see, Adultery is when a third party enters a relationship. Whether or not you are in bed with someone, Lust will lead you on a journey of self-satisfaction. That journey can begin with a touch, a smile or a caress. Sex is a journey from beginning to end, from start to finish.

Each time you feel a little pat on you from the other twin that says: "You deserve this, you deserve the secret touch, the smile, caress, sex. After all, you don't get it at home". This is Pride talking! How blind are we not to see it?

Second Samuel, chapter 11, has a powerful story about David, whom God told the Prophet Samuel to anoint king over Israel. God chose this young lad, who at the time was minding sheep. He purposely hand-picked him from among his brothers and through the prophet said, "You will be King over Israel!" He rose in rank under King Saul and watched and learned the 'ins and outs' of royalty. David was so respected as commander of the army of Israel that within its ranks a unit of specialist soldiers was formed, called "The Mighty Men" (2 Samuel 23:8-39). This unit became his loyal bodyguard, for whom no deed was too difficult. They defeated the undefeatable! These were the kind of men David hung out with. David had begun as a shepherd but was now a warrior!

David had everything at his side: God, a wife who was the daughter of King Saul, children, a palace, an army, and a nation that sang his praises every time he returned from battle. He lacked for nothing.

However, David did not see that another enemy, Lust, was making arrangements. It was setting the scene, creating the props for the stage of his soon-coming fall. It was only a matter of time before the clock would chime to set the events in motion. Let's go into this story...

2 Samuel 11 v 1

"And it came to pass, after the year had expired, at the time when kings go forth to battle, that David sent Joab, and his servant with him, and all Israel; and they destroyed the children of Ammon and besieged Rabbah. But David tarried at Jerusalem."

"But" is a very small word, yet even when used normally it changes the storyline. For instance, someone might say, "I found a stack of money today, but…" When you hear that "but" straight away you think, "This storyline is about to change!" "But" is a powerful word that informs us something has taken place – or is about to take place – that should not.

The last, short sentence in this verse reads: "But David tarried at Jerusalem." This indicates that David should have been somewhere else, and the first sentence in the verse tells us where he should have been. "At the time when kings go forth to battle…David sent Joab." As the commander in chief of the army of Israel, David should have been at the forefront of battle, leading his comrades, but instead he stayed home.

As teenagers we hear that rules are there to be broken, that it's OK to bend the rules a little, to tell that little white lie. Sure, everyone does it. God will understand. Hey, God understood so much that He sent Jesus! There is no excuse for us. A second excuse would require a second sacrifice of the Lamb – and that's just not going to happen! David lost his sharp cutting edge. It can also happen to us. We can find ourselves in a place where our sharpness in the Spirit is dulled and our attitude stinks. When this happens, we send other people to do what we were meant to be doing. But God has set down rules. He has established perimeters. We know them as laws, or "truths" as the Church calls them. These truths are not there for our comfort but for our protection. Where there are electric wires there is also a sign that shows a guy being fried! It's not the sign that will fry us but the electric wires. The sign is a warning. It's the same with the truths of the Bible and God's laws: like that warning sign, they are there to warn us not to cross the line, for in doing so we may get fried!

The basis of this story is that there is a time when kings should go forth to battle, and to us that time is the warning sign. In this sense, David should have been doing what the sign said – "It's time to go out to the battle." But instead David decided to take the day off and we all know what happens when we take time off when we shouldn't. The same thing happens that happened to Adam and Eve: the serpent will enter through the hole that we have left open and bite us! David, having set aside his responsibility to be where he should be, was now in a place where he should not be. Can you guess what happens when you're in a place where you should not be? Let's see...

2 Samuel 11 v 2

"And it came to pass in an evening tide, that David arose from off his bed, and walked upon the roof of the king's house: and from the roof he saw a woman washing herself; and the woman was very beautiful to look upon."

Do you think that David had just risen after waking from sleep, and while strolling on the flat roof of the palace, just happened to eye a woman washing herself? The Bible says, "*...the woman was very beautiful to look upon.*" This means she ticked all the right boxes for David, and even though he had fought giants and won wars, a new and different enemy, Lust, rose within him.

You may ask "How do you know that David lusted?" Quite simply, the Bible says...

3"*And David sent and enquired after the woman. And one said, Is not this Bathsheba, the daughter of Eliam, the wife of Uriah the Hittite?*

4*And David sent messengers, and took her; and she came in unto him, and he lay with her; for she was purified from her uncleanness: and she returned unto her house."*

The Bible describes Bathsheba as beautiful, but an underlying factor was that her name meant "Daughter of oath." Her name speaks of loyalty of character. Likewise, loyalty was one of David's characteristics. During David's time serving in the court of King Saul's palace, Saul tried to kill him more times than we care to mention; and yet David had remained loyal to the point that when the opportunity arose to slay Saul (1Sam. 24 v 1 – 10) his loyalty to the throne was greater than the death sentence Saul had placed upon him. This loyalty to God's anointed king was why David refused to take Saul's life when he could have done so quite easily.

As the "Daughter of oath" Bathsheba was committed to God, for at the time David saw her she was bathing. That's how the translators of the King James Version put it. But a more careful study of the Hebrew will show that she was actually in the act of finishing her purification rites after her menstruation period had ended. Under the Law of Israel, once a woman had stopped menstruating she would bathe for seven days (Lev. 15 v 19 – 30). On the eighth day, the final day of her purification, she would have brought a sacrifice of burnt offerings to the priest.

Take another look at verse four...

4"And David sent messengers, and took her; and she came in unto him, and he lay with her; for she was purified from her uncleanness: and she returned unto her house."

When the Bible mentions messengers one thing you must realise is that they are not on an outing or a picnic but a mission, and that each mission has an end in view. For these guys the mission was to "take" Bathsheba to the royal palace. Bathsheba had very little choice in this matter. The King of Israel had seen her and had wanted her, and to refuse a king meant certain death.

After David killed Goliath, Saul gave his daughter Michal to David in marriage. But even the majesty of a king's daughter was not enough. This Adulterous Spirit was now in play with David, and the king had fallen under its spell. Lust not denied has no restraint!

David was now on a path that would end bitterly for him. But that was far from his thoughts as he took Bathsheba into his bedroom and slept with her. The Hunter within him was satisfied for the time being.

Since the patterns and types in the Bible portray the realities of the New Testament, could it be that this Old Testament story was actually a warning for the Church? Let me explain...

The Old Testament was a shadow of the New Testament, and what the people of the Old Testament did naturally we can do spiritually.

In the matter of Adultery, the Old Testament teaches, "Do not commit Adultery!" It had to be a physical act for it to be judged Adultery. The New Testament teaches, "If you look on a woman to lust after her you commit adultery!" On the New Testament basis, one does not have to have sex to commit adultery; all one has to do is lust for her. A higher law for a higher kingdom!

Since the spiritual kingdom is higher than that of the natural kingdom, are you aware that when you are born-again of the Spirit you become a king under God?

The Bible says in Revelation 1 v 6

"And hath made us kings and priests unto God and his Father; to him be glory and dominion forever and ever. Amen."

God chose David to be crowned king, and this Scripture clearly states that God has made us kings as well. Could it be possible that God is trying to show the Church something but the Church is not seeing it?

Could it be that those in the Church, who have been chosen, anointed and made kings by God have this Adulterous Spirit, and that Lust might still be in the Church?

As we take a further look into this Adulterous Spirit and its ways, you will come to see that what we often see as our goal, is not the goal of the Adulterous Spirit.

Chapter 12

The Three Letter Word is Not the End Goal

Unfaithfulness results from an affair, and when this happens it is normally accepted that those involved have only one thing on their minds, and that is the three letter word Sex! But what if sex is not the end goal? What if it is rather Lust that seeks to take you out of your boundaries into another setting?

Lust started away back in the Garden of Eden, when God set boundaries for Adam and Eve. God laid out His will in saying you shall do this and you shall not do that. These were boundaries! Then satan came as a serpent and caused them to lust after that which was not theirs – the tree of the knowledge of good and evil. Satan tempted them to go outside their boundary, and when they did they fell under the spell of Lust.

In John 10:10 the Bible says, "*The thief comes only to steal, to kill, to destroy!*" Have you noticed it does not mention that three letter word Sex? The reason it does not mention sex is because sex is not the final result that Lust seeks after. The two brothers of satan known as Adultery and Lust are only using the affair as camouflage! What then is their real reason? Are you ready for this?

The mission of these evil twins is to destroy you, and for them to accomplish this, they will seek to remove what you have, expose what you have done, snare you and bring you to a place you never dreamt of – a condition the Bible calls DESTROYED.

If you have fallen into Lust, it is not just about sex; it can also be lust for power or lust for people to always be pleased with you. Please realise that all lust is based on deception, and if this is the path you are now on, you must know that God has a way out for you, that He has made a way of escape. God will not rest until you come back to where you belong – the foot of the Cross. But before you come to the foot of the Cross you need to have a revelation as to how the enemy deceived you and got a hold on you, or you will drift back into deception. Now, back to the story of David...

5 *"And the woman conceived, and sent and told David, and said, I am with child."*

Such was the power of the lust that ensnared David, he may have thought to himself: Nice girl, I will have some of that! But Lust had more than sex in mind for David, for it knew that if it could tempt him into Adultery it could expose the heart of David. So Lust captured David's emotions to the point where David could not settle until he had Bathsheba in his bedroom. Forget the fact that she was another man's wife. Forget the fact that she was the wife of one of his best and most loyal comrades in battle. And don't even begin to think that Bathsheba has not long finished her menstruation, and that her womb is crying out to conceive! All systems are green to go! Don't even contemplate that one of the greatest prophets in the world has earlier in his life chosen him from among his brothers and said – "You're God's man for the hour!" So many things in front of David screamed "Red light! Red light! Do not cross this line!" And yet when Lust captures a person there's no place for patience; it's all about the speed of the hunt and the gratification it seeks. Lust had set David up for a fall. The great commander of Israel's army had been led into an ambush.

I would imagine that after David had sent Bathsheba home he was still thinking about her. In his mind he could still feel her in his arms, and every so often he would look across to where he had first seen her, just to remind himself of that secret time they'd had together. Guilt may at times have gripped him because of what he had done, but then somehow he would have dismissed the feeling, thinking maybe that God had not seen it and that even if he had, He was sure to forgive.

Then there was a knock on the palace door, and in came one of his officials, David straightened himself up in his seat and tried to come back to earth. His thoughts about Bathsheba left a sick feeling in his gut but he didn't know why. The official bowed and spoke. "Bathsheba is with child!"

Fear, panic, dread! What will happen now? What will the people think? What will I do? Question after question flooded through his mind. The act he had done in secret was now about to be exposed in the open! Have you ever been in that place?

The cover-up that happened in Eden after the Fall was about to be replayed. David thought, I need to cover this up. So he gave an order: "Send me Uriah, the husband of Bathsheba."

6 "*And David sent to Joab, saying, Send me Uriah the Hittite. And Joab sent Uriah to David.*

7 *And when Uriah was come unto him, David demanded of him how Joab did, and how the people did, and how the war prospered.*

8 *And David said to Uriah, Go down to thy house, and wash thy feet. And Uriah departed out of the king's house, and there followed him a mess of meat from the king.*

9 *But Uriah slept at the door of the king's house with all the servants of his lord, and went not down to his house.*"

Everything would now be alright, David must have thought. Wouldn't it?

Chapter 13

A set of Triplets called 'Do'

The quicker we learn that nothing good can come from the flesh the better it will be for us. Flesh is a wild beast that knows only how to fend for itself, for it is interested only in self.

David had fallen from the ways of God into the snare of the Adulterous Spirit. His communication with Heaven was down and out of order, and he was now well advanced in making plans through the arm of the flesh. No longer was he consulting with God.

Are you aware that bad things happen to innocent people? In this story the innocent party is Uriah, the husband of Bathsheba, a loyal soldier to King David and an honourable man to his comrades in arms. They didn't come much better than Uriah.

Uriah earned his income as a soldier for King David. This meant that for weeks and months he left the safety of his home to dice with death confronting the enemies of Israel. He fought every battle for his hero King David and for the safety of his wife back home. Little did he know that the very one for whom he was willing to lay down his life daily was preparing to take his life in more ways than one.

David, now knowing that Bathsheba was pregnant, realised that he must now cover his mistake and what better way to cover a woman getting pregnant than to make it look as though the wife's husband was responsible? But how to do that if the husband is not at home? No problem for David the king; simply grant the husband leave and send him home to his wife!

I can imagine Uriah on the battlefield, splattered with the blood of David's enemies, and Joab, David's general, approaching him and saying, "King David wants to see you!" While travelling back from the battlefield he must have given some thought as to why his king had requested his presence; and when at last he stood before the throne must have wondered: Why am I here?

Have you ever sat in front of someone who is trying to say something but not actually saying it? Or you just know they are trying to set you up? You and I are blessed because we have the Holy Spirit, and listening to Him we can come into an awareness of who is for us and who is against us. This can happen without us even sitting in front of them. But Uriah did not have the Holy Spirit in him, and his trust was in those whom God had put over him.

Uriah was in the great room of the palace and David was quizzing him about the battle – how was it going? But little did Uriah know that the true motive of the meeting was not about a natural battle but a spiritual battle that David had already lost, one that he now needed to cover up.

Then David made a suggestion: "Go back home, bathe, and rest for a while with your wife." After being away so long it would be only right for Uriah to go home, have a nice long bath, and then enjoy his wife. And to help him along, a parcel of food would be sent with him to celebrate his homecoming. I think very few guys would have turned down time home with a beautiful wife after being told by the King to take the rest of the week off on full pay; and, for a bonus: a parcel of the King's food! Most soldiers would say that King David had ticked all their boxes and would happily head home to have pleasure with their wives with a hamper from the king! Yes, most soldiers would, but not the one told to do it. Not Uriah.

9 "But Uriah slept at the door of the king's house with all the servants of his lord, and went not down to his house.

10 And when they had told David, saying, Uriah went not down unto his house, David said unto Uriah, Camest thou not from thy journey? Why then didst thou not go down unto thine house?

11 And Uriah said unto David, The ark, and Israel, and Judah, abide in tents; and my lord Joab, and the servants of my lord, are encamped in the open fields; shall I then go into mine house, to eat and to drink, and to lie with my wife? As thou livest, and as thy soul liveth, I will not do this thing."

When David heard Uriah say "I will not do this thing" he must have thought, "I was like that once: nothing came before doing what was right before God. I sought God's Presence once, I stood and fought giants once, and I knew how to praise God!"

But now David, who do you see when you look in the mirror? The person who started out well? Or the person who veered off along the way? If you are like David at this point and cannot bring yourself to admit that you have done wrong, the path of error continues like a water slide that will only take you one way and that is down! David was now on the way down to destruction, and it would be those closest to him that would feel the wrath that would follow.

12 *"And David said to Uriah, Tarry here today also, and tomorrow I will let thee depart. So Uriah abode in Jerusalem that day, and the morrow.*

13 *And when David had called him, he did eat and drink before him; and he made him drunk: and at even he went out to lie on his bed with the servants of his lord, but went not down to his house.*

14 *And it came to pass in the morning, that David wrote a letter to Joab, and sent it by the hand of Uriah.*

15 *And he wrote in the letter, saying, Set ye Uriah in the forefront of the hottest battle, and retire ye from him, that he may be smitten, and die.*

16 *And it came to pass, when Joab observed the city that he assigned Uriah unto a place where he knew that valiant men were.*

17 *And the men of the city went out, and fought with Joab: and there fell some of the people of the servants of David; and Uriah the Hittite died also."*

I am about to introduce you to one of the most important questions you will ever be asked, In fact, I would say that each day before you make a decision you should ask yourself this question. Are you ready? Then let me introduce you to a set of triplets called "Do"!

When you meet them they will ask, "Why do you do what you do?"

There is a motive behind almost everything that we do. If we eat food it is usually because we are hungry. If we exercise it is to become fit. If we wash the car it's probably because it's dirty. If we go to work it's because we need money. If we go to the doctor it is because something is wrong. And if you are having an affair it is because..? I will leave you to answer that.

You must uncover your true motive, because if you don't what motivates you can bring death of a friendship, the death of a marriage, the death of a promising career. Never be scared to meet the "Do" triplets and answer them honestly when they ask, "Why do you do what you do?"

If David had only done that, several lives would have been saved and a wife would not have transgressed. Be sure to keep the triplets on hand, because they may well save your life!

Uriah travelled back to the battlefield without realising that he was carrying his own death warrant. He gave the orders to Joab, and was instructed by the general to go to a place in the battle from which he would never return. David had set up Uriah to be killed.

18 "Then Joab sent and told David all the things concerning the war;

19 And charged the messenger, saying, when thou hast made an end of telling the matters of the war unto the king,

20 And if so be that the king's wrath arise and he say unto thee, Wherefore approached ye so nigh unto the city when ye did fight? Knew ye not that they would shoot from the wall?

21 Who smote Abimelech the son of Jerubbesheth? Did not a woman cast a piece of a millstone upon him from the wall that he died in Thebez? Why went ye nigh the wall? Then say thou, Thy servant Uriah the Hittite is dead also.

22 So the messenger went, and came and shewed David all that Joab had sent him for.

23 And the messenger said unto David, Surely the men prevailed against us, and came out unto us into the field, and we were upon them even unto the entering of the gate.

24 And the shooters shot from off the wall upon thy servants; and some of the king's servants be dead, and thy servant Uriah the Hittite is dead also.

25 Then David said unto the messenger, Thus shalt thou say unto Joab, Let not this thing displease thee, for the sword devoureth one as well as another: make thy battle more strong against the city, and overthrow it: and encourage thou him."

Have you ever allowed the expression "God understands" to settle within you? I remember a day when all I heard from people who came into the shop were two words: "God understands!" Some of these people had been on the Christian road for many years. As they chatted, it seemed to me that they had met a different God to the one I had come to know. They spoke of how it was OK to tell a white lie, to evade paying your bills, to have another partner on the side, to have sex before marriage… and the list went on. I'm sure you have heard the same excuses. "It's OK to evade paying bills; after all others don't pay theirs". "It's OK to have another partner on the side when you are lonely with your existing one". "It's OK to have sex before marriage, since you are going to marry them anyway". As I challenged these people, the main statement that each one of them said was, "God understands!"

Although as a young Christian who at the time knew very little of the Bible, I closed the shop that night actually feeling dirty. Like Abraham, I looked up into the sky more than a little confused, thinking that surely those who had been on the road a lot longer than me, some even leaders in the body of Christ -- could not be wrong! I asked God, "Do you understand?" I will never forget what happened next: tears filled my eyes as an inward voice said, *"I understood so well that I sent Jesus!"* Whaaa! Those words almost blew me over! They set me free! Jesus came, and because He did we have no excuse for lies and deception. How many in the Body of Christ are walking in deception thinking that because God understands they can rip someone off; that they can do whatever they like without feeling guilty?

My friend, God may indeed forgive, but the consequences of sin are another thing, and David was about to find out.

Chapter 14

The Truth is No Lie

[26]"And when the wife of Uriah heard that Uriah her husband was dead, she mourned for her husband.

[27]And when the mourning was past, David sent and fetched her to his house, and she became his wife, and bare him a son. But the thing that David had done displeased the LORD."

Like those teachers of the Law who heard Jesus teach, many church members today are so far away from the Truth that they would not see it – even if it was right under their nose. When are we going to come to the Light and let it shine right through us, exposing the mire and dirt hidden in our hearts?

In John 16 v 13, Jesus says: "*Howbeit when he, the Spirit of truth, is come* (and according to Acts 2:1-4 the Holy Spirit came into the Church on the day of Pentecost), *he will guide you into all truth...*"

Notice that it does not say: When the spirit of deception comes it will guide you into all deception. Neither does it say that when the spirit of lies comes it will guide you into all lies.

It clearly states, "*When he, the Spirit of truth, is come, he will guide you into all truth...*" What a mighty revelation for us to walk in! God is Truth, which means that no matter where He leads you and no matter who He sends you to, and whomever He sends you, Truth must be clearly seen in the call; there must be no deception in any shape or form.

Take this as good advice! If you are on the road to deception and are telling lies in order to deceive, God is NOT down that road, and the quicker you reverse from where the lies and deception are taking you, the sooner you will feel a fresh touch from the Master. If the journey you are now on is causing you to cover your tracks, then note that the traffic lights at the end of this road you are on are flashing RED! You need to stop NOW and go in the opposite direction before it is too late!

This is why the Church of Jesus Christ is in need of true prophets. Where are the prophets that can see into people's lives and uncover the secret sins that are hidden in the hearts of Church people?

Listen carefully! Never be afraid of a true prophet, because God reveals to heal, to direct, to bless! It is the devil who exposes and destroys. There is a BIG difference!

I have seen prophets call out people and publicly tell them that they are in adultery or suchlike. Their partner in marriage knew nothing until the whole thing was put in public view by the prophet, leaving the partner stripped of dignity and emotionally distraught. Personally, I do not agree with this practice of stripping people bare in public. I think that if Jesus came into church in our bad days and pointed out our sins before everyone, we would run a mile and probably never go back to that church. What is done to one should be done to all.

Through the examples of John Hamilton and Alec Schofield, two men of God I was blessed to have speak into in my life, I learnt that the gifts, when used with wisdom and understanding, bring great reward to the kingdom. Without these they can be very destructive.

When a true prophet comes into the midst of a people, he comes not to expose and to humiliate. That is the work of the devil. He comes to fix, to adjust, to mend, to direct, to sharpen you in the Spirit.

A prophet's insight is not unlike that of your local doctor. You go to him for an annual check-up, especially as you grow older. As you enter the surgery to be examined your heart begins to beat faster! Thoughts shoot through your mind. Will he find anything wrong with me? The doctor asks, "Can I examine you?" and of course you agree. He runs the usual checks and you wait, heart nearly bouncing out of your body, and then he says, "You are fine, see you next year!" That's what it's like when you ask a prophet to pray for you. You are really asking him to give you a spiritual check-up, to see if there is any part that is not lining up with what God would want.

What if the doctor were to say, "I have found something but we can treat it"? That is like the prophet pinpointing something and then giving you some direction. The prophet does not come to destroy you but to help you. Just as some things a doctor tells you are hard to accept, the same applies when a prophet confronts you and identifies your problem. But listen carefully to what he is saying. I have never in my life had an injection that did not hurt, yet each one was given to help me to become whole in body. As it is in the natural, so is it in the spiritual!

And for me a prophet is more important than a doctor, because a doctor does his best to keep you healthy during this life, but the prophet's words not only bring present direction, they also prepare you for the next life.

King David had forgotten that God still had prophets, and a prophet called Nathan not only had the gift but the wisdom and the understanding to go with it. Let's watch the story unfold as Nathan drops the bait and David, like a fish, takes the hook. This reveals to me that God is great at fishing, and knows exactly how to reel us in!

2 Samuel 12

1 *"And the LORD sent Nathan unto David. And he came unto him, and said unto him, there were two men in one city; the one rich, and the other poor.*

2 *The rich man had exceeding many flocks and herds:*

3 *But the poor man had nothing, save one little ewe lamb, which he had bought and nourished up: and it grew up together with him, and with his children; it did eat of his own meat, and drank of his own cup, and lay in his bosom, and was unto him as a daughter.*

4 *And there came a traveller unto the rich man, and he spared to take of his own flock and of his own herd, to dress for the wayfaring man that was come unto him; but took the poor man's lamb, and dressed it for the man that was come to him.*

5 *And David's anger was greatly kindled against the man; and he said to Nathan, As the LORD liveth, the man that hath done this thing shall surely die:*

6 *And he shall restore the lamb fourfold, because he did this thing, and because he had no pity.*

7 *And Nathan said to David, Thou art the man. Thus saith the LORD*

God of Israel, I anointed thee king over Israel, and I delivered thee out of the hand of Saul;

[8]And I gave thee thy master's house, and thy master's wives into thy bosom, and gave thee the house of Israel and of Judah; and if that had been too little, I would moreover have given unto thee such and such things.

[9]Wherefore hast thou despised the commandment of the LORD, to do evil in his sight? thou hast killed Uriah the Hittite with the sword, and hast taken his wife to be thy wife, and hast slain him with the sword of the children of Ammon.

[10]Now therefore the sword shall never depart from thine house; because thou hast despised me, and hast taken the wife of Uriah the Hittite to be thy wife.

[11]Thus saith the LORD, Behold, I will raise up evil against thee out of thine own house, and I will take thy wives before thine eyes, and give them unto thy neighbour, and he shall lie with thy wives in the sight of this sun.

[12]For thou didst it secretly: but I will do this thing before all Israel, and before the sun.

[13]And David said unto Nathan, I have sinned against the LORD. And Nathan said unto David, The LORD also hath put away thy sin; thou shalt not die.

[14]Howbeit, because by this deed thou hast given great occasion to the enemies of the LORD to blaspheme, the child also that is born unto thee shall surely die."

God loves us to the degree that He is willing to walk with us, talk with us, and have fellowship with us – as He did with Adam. Nothing is more fulfilling than a relationship with the Holy Spirit, in which He is more real than a person who sits beside you would be.

Even though David had done a serious wrong, his judgements in other matters were still accurate. When the prophet Nathan told King David a story that paralleled what he had done, the king made the correct judgement, but in making that judgement he brought judgement upon himself. Remember, what you sow is what you reap! (Galatians 6:7)

Jesus said in Matthew 7:

[2] *"For with what judgment ye judge, ye shall be judged: and with what measure ye mete, it shall be measured to you again."*

On hearing Nathan's story, David pronounced that the punishment for the man who had committed the offence would be death, and that restoration would be paid to the man against whom the offence had been perpetrated.

Not knowing that he was the one in Nathan's story, the king unwittingly judged that he himself was guilty and deserved a death sentence. I wonder if he would have pronounced the same sentence if he had known that it was he who had committed the crime.

Maybe what we can all learn from this is that when we see or hear that someone is fallen, we should not crucify the person, because Jesus has already been crucified for sin. We should rather embrace them, knowing that but for God's grace we could have gone down sin's path. I would say to those who have already taken this path: you know how lonely it is, and how much you still thirst for what God had for you. You know what it's like to be torn in two, wanting God on one hand and adultery on the other. Some people will ask, "How could you do that, being a Christian?" My response is quite simple. I think that T D Jakes explains it very well when he says that if a pig falls into a mud pond it just enjoys it. It doesn't just lie in it but rolls in it. A mud pond is a pig's paradise! But when a lamb passes a mud pond and falls in, something inside of it knows straight away that it is not made for mud, and it struggles with all its strength to get out of the mud. One likes being in filth and the other knows that there is something better. Can I ask you this question: Are you happy rolling around in the filth, or do you believe that there is something better?

Do you really enjoy the lies and the deception? What of the unfaithfulness to your marriage partner and to God? Or is it that each time you enter this path you feel a sickness in your stomach, knowing that your spiritual and moral radar is warning that you are stepping out of God's covering and into enemy territory? My friend, since you had the courage to read this book, then I can say that either you are a lamb, seeking to come out of the mud, or that you know of a lamb that is caught in the mud! Either way, Jesus has paid a costly price to save that lamb. The least we can do is to listen to God's voice through the interference we've been hearing. When we do, his instructions will be pure and simple, and if followed will make you whole. His word to you is "Come!"

Listen and please understand: some of us have been where you are, in sin and darkness, far away from God. But think of how it is when dirt hardens on you and you slip into that bath or shower and feel the cleansing of that pure water! There is nothing like it! Your life can be like that after a fresh cleansing from the Master. In the next chapter I will share more of my story...

Chapter 15

When Your Trousers Don't Fit

During my early adult years I lived in what the Bible calls "gross darkness". Iniquity had been passed down to me, and when this happens there's not much choice in the matter. The only answer to iniquity is Jesus. But, unfortunately, due to "The Troubles" in our land, some of us had no choice as to how we grew up; and maybe it was the same for you, in that you had no choice of who or what you were involved with.

I can tell you from experience that the darker your path has been, the greater the Light you need God to reveal to you. You know why? The greater the pain the greater the antidote needs to be.

It's a great sadness to me that in today's Church we have people who are suffering from turmoil and they are told to keep singing, keep confessing, keep believing; and most end up going to the grave after fighting the darkness to their last breath.

This book is about helping you get back onto the path that Jesus has for you. It's about helping you to see and understand that God has already put under your feet the things that are trying to destroy you.

We must come to a realization that we can jump into the water of the Holy Spirit and be continuously bathed in Him, which will bring a new fragrance that will dwell upon us. The Bible calls this to be hid with Christ (Anointing) in God. (Col:3:3)

I had come to know the Lord early in life but later backslid. It was during those ten years of darkness that I never thought I would ever see age twenty-one. Darkness that you could feel, darkness so intense that when I looked at someone they said that death was looking at them through my eyes. It brought fear to most people I met. I was out of control and away from the Master. But I thank God that even though I had walked away from Him, He had never walked away from me! His hand still protected me and His finger still directed me. God would soon impact my life to such a degree that, like Jacob, I would never be the same again.

I had come so far down the road that I realised I could never go back up it again by myself. It was as though the road had become a maze, yet in my pride I still thought that I would be OK. I know what I am doing, I told myself, and I can get out of it! But like Samson there comes a point when we are caught in the trap and it's too late! Yes, God can still rescue us, because He is like that; but how much better if we had never gone down that road! How much pain and heartache we and our loved ones would have missed!

I was raised in a church until I was sixteen. I had memorized the Scriptures and Catechisms every Sunday. But even after learning both, I never really understood them. For instance, in one Catechism they ask: Why was man created? Answer: To glorify God and to enjoy Him forever!

Yes, I was able to answer, "To glorify God!" But as a sixteen-year-old, did I understand it? No!

Another Scripture I had to learn was; wait for it -- Jeremiah 33 v 8 *"And I will cleanse them from all their iniquity, whereby they have sinned against me; and I will pardon all their iniquities, whereby they have sinned, and whereby they have transgressed against me."*

I remember asking the Sunday school teacher "What do the words "iniquity" and "transgressed" mean?" She said, "I am the one who asks the questions, not you, and that is not one of the questions!" Is it any wonder God hates the traditions of the elders – that which has been handed down but is not understood? It's what I call religion!

I had been raised in what could be called a "dry" church, in which no expression other than that taught by rote and repeated by habit was allowed. Other kinds of expression were simply unacceptable. But if any church member attended a soccer match, expressing excitement was quite acceptable! Clapping of hands to music or singing was not allowed in the church; they would say that was "of the world". But if they went to a concert they clapped excitedly. Moreover, it was totally disrespectful for a child to look around to see what was happening. No matter what, the rules had to be obeyed!

In my early twenties my Mum would constantly ask me to go to a church, but I kept putting off until I just had to go to stop her moaning at me. But when I went to my first Pentecostal church meeting, little did I know what an experience it was going to be, compared with the kind of church I had been raised in.

The people smiled from ear to ear and gave me the impression they were floating on air. Never had so many strangers shook my hand so vigorously and said "Welcome!" So much so that I became a bit nervous – was it a set up?

Then the music started, but hold on, there was more playing than an organ! Surely this could not be acceptable to God, I thought. At least, that was what I had been taught during my younger days in the other church. Anything other than an organ meant one was in the world system. Then I heard the bang, bang, bang of drums and what a racket! The guy playing the drums didn't have a note in his head but was happy as long as he was making a noise! I thought: surely God could not be in this place! But wait till I tell you this: a woman took to the floor, dancing and waving a tambourine! That was it for me; it confirmed that all this was not of God. Surely God was not into dancing, especially in His Church. I was outraged at what I was seeing and hearing!

After they had sung about three choruses, silence fell. I remember asking, "What is happening now?" only to be told by Mum, "Be quiet!" (That put me in my place!) When the meeting quieted down a feeling of warmth came all over me and surrounded me. Then it got more and more intense. So much so that I reached over and felt the radiators to see if they were on and they were cold to the point of being frozen. My mind began to take a beating as a result of the heat that now surrounded me.

Then a guy spoke in a foreign language, and part of me wanted to run out of the building, because my religious upbringing had taught me that tongues were no longer on the earth, and that if you heard them they were of the devil. By now I was thinking, Is this scary or what?

The other half of me felt as though a magnet was holding me in place, so that I couldn't move. But the strangest thing of all then happened. I had a sort of intuition inside me that whatever was going to happen next was about me, and yet I had no clue what that was going to be.

An interpretation of the tongues came next from a lady at the front, and I want you to listen closely, as it were, to the words that came from God, because they may also speak to you.

"Come away with Me, come away with Me, saith the Lord. For I have waited for this time, I have waited for this opportunity. Yea, you have questioned am I real, and I say to you; Before you were born I knew all about you. Yea, I know your down-fallings, I know the secrets of your heart; but I say unto you, Come away with me. Say "Yes" to my will, "Yes" to your God. I say again, Come away with Me, come away with me, saith your God!"

When those words ended the heat that surrounded me lifted and the meeting continued. I can say that the words that were spoken while that heat was over me had stuck to me like glue. It felt as if I could not separate myself from them. Something had happened. The seed of Christ had germinated in me! Within hours I surrendered my life to God, never to be the same again.

This is what God wants for you, too: He wants you to have an experience in Him that will cause you to outgrow the spiritual trousers that you're now wearing. Like an eight-year-old that has grown to a twenty-year-old, the trousers that once fit so well cannot even be pulled up over the legs! We all know what it's like to outgrow what once fitted comfortably, and to go up a few sizes as we mature in this life; and it's the same as we mature spiritually. We need to outgrow what 'was' to live in to what "is" if we are to seek what "is to come" in God.

Revelation 1:4 "*...from him* (Jesus) *which* ***is****, and which* ***was****, and which* ***is to come****...*"

You need to live in God's "now" rather than in your past experiences! "I remember what God did" needs to become "I know what God is doing"! Memories are good but present-day experiences are imperative if we're to live in the "now" of God! God is waiting for you, and His message to you is the same as it was to me: "Come away with Me.." Reach out your heart and your hand to Him and the Master will straighten the crooked road you're on – just as He made David's crooked path straight.

Chapter 16

When Death Comes Knocking

At this point a virus had gotten into David's hard drive and his life was now in a downward spiral; but God was about to update the damaged drive of his heart with an antivirus through a prophet.

2 Samuel 11

[12] *"For thou didst it secretly: but I will do this thing before all Israel, and before the sun.*

[13] *And David said unto Nathan, I have sinned against the LORD. And Nathan said unto David, The LORD also hath put away thy sin; thou shalt not die.*

[14] *Howbeit, because by this deed thou hast given great occasion to the enemies of the LORD to blaspheme, the child also that is born unto thee shall surely die."*

2 Samuel 12

[15] *"And Nathan departed unto his house. And the LORD struck the child that Uriah's wife bare unto David, and it was very sick."*

The path to wholeness must first begin with an admission of what is wrong. David realised that if he were to find wholeness again he would have to confess that he had sinned by doing a great wrong. Thus the King of Israel bowed his knees to the God of Israel and, surrendering himself afresh, gave voice from his inner being words that would become Psalm 51:

[1] *"Have mercy upon me, O God, according to thy loving-kindness: according unto the multitude of thy tender mercies blot out my transgressions.*

[2] *Wash me thoroughly from mine iniquity, and cleanse me from my sin.*

[3] *For I acknowledge my transgressions: and my sin is ever before me.*

4Against thee, thee only, have I sinned, and done this evil in thy sight: that thou mightiest be justified when thou speakest, and be clear when thou judgest.

5Behold, I was shapen in iniquity; and in sin did my mother conceive me.

6Behold, thou desirest truth in the inward parts: and in the hidden part thou shalt make me to know wisdom.

7Purge me with hyssop, and I shall be clean: wash me, and I shall be whiter than snow.

8Make me to hear joy and gladness; that the bones which thou hast broken may rejoice.

9Hide thy face from my sins, and blot out all mine iniquities.

10Create in me a clean heart, O God; and renew a right spirit within me.

11Cast me not away from thy presence; and take not thy Holy Spirit from me.

12Restore unto me the joy of thy salvation; and uphold me with thy free spirit.

13Then will I teach transgressors thy ways; and sinners shall be converted unto thee.

14Deliver me from bloodguiltiness, O God, thou God of my salvation: and my tongue shall sing aloud of thy righteousness.

15O Lord, open thou my lips; and my mouth shall shew forth thy praise.

16For thou desirest not sacrifice; else would I give it: thou delightest not in burnt offering.

17The sacrifices of God are a broken spirit: a broken and a contrite heart, O God, thou wilt not despise.

18Do good in thy good pleasure unto Zion: build thou the walls of Jerusalem.

19Then shalt thou be pleased with the sacrifices of righteousness, with burnt offering and whole burnt offering: then shall they offer bullocks upon thine altar.

Imagine the sight of the prophet Nathan standing before David's throne and delivering Heaven's courtroom verdict: "You have been found guilty of transgression." Echoing in David's mind was the thought: I knew what came into my mind to do was wrong, and yet I did it.

When a transgression comes to light there is a consequence. It's like telling a child not to put its hand in the fire and they still do it. Some people would say that it was the fire's fault that the child was burnt. But if the child had done what it was told its hand would not have been burnt. The consequence of its disobedience was a burnt hand.

David had done the same – except that in his case he was the one who put his hand into the fire, in a manner of speaking, but it was the child that got burnt. Since it was the innocent party we might ask, "Why did the child have to die?"

The key is found in 2 Samuel 12:14

[14] *"Howbeit, because by this deed thou hast given great occasion to the enemies of the LORD to blaspheme, the child also that is born unto thee shall surely die".*

If God had not judged David, Israel's enemies would have criticized it and blasphemed its God. Likewise, if there are no consequences to murder, murderers in general would feel free to kill whoever they wished! But when they know that once caught they will receive a life sentence in prison, or even the death penalty, they think twice before committing murder. The justice in God's judgement is that since David's act brought death to Uriah, the consequence will be that his new-born child must die.

One of the most difficult things in life is for people to admit they were wrong, that they have failed, that a decision they made was incorrect.

It's only when we come to a place of brokenness that God can move in our lives. The knees of our strong will have to bow before we are prepared to admit to God, "I was wrong!"

Remember that God cannot heal until we admit that we need to be healed. God cannot forgive until we admit that we need His forgiveness. God cannot restore if we are unwilling to admit our failings. With this in mind, the following will bring a basic understanding of one's spirit, soul and body.

1 Thessalonians 5:23 informs us that each one of us has a spirit, a soul and a body.

A Spirit – To the natural eye a spirit is invisible, but when God opens our spiritual eyes we are able to see into the spiritual realm. The Bible tells the story of Elisha asking the Lord to open the eyes of a young man (2 Kings 6:17). Elisha was not referring to his natural eyes because the young man had already seen the enemy that surrounded them. He was referring to his spiritual eyes, and when God opened them he saw a host of angels far greater in number than the enemy. (The invisible sees the invisible.) You are a spirit, housed in a body, and were created to commune with the invisible God! (1 Timothy 1:17)

A Soul – Just as a computer has a hard drive, we too have a hard drive that stores memory. It works out possibilities from the information stored, and this allows us to interact with the natural realm.

A Body – Not too many have seen a computer without its housing (the metal covering that surrounds the system). That housing covers and protects the important parts of the computer's internal settings. The housing can be likened to our body, or as many call it, our earth suit. When we die our earth suits falls away but our soul and spirit continue, for they are eternal and that which is eternal can never die.

Many times we fall away or swerve off course, only to be sorry for what we have done. But this kind of sorrow is on the human level. When we realise that there is a spiritual world which is more real than the world that can be seen, we will seek the spirit life more than we seek the natural life. Fulfilling a temporal role is not as important as fulfilling the eternal purpose.

On hearing Nathan the prophet's words, the king knew that his soul had led him to commit adultery with Bathsheba. The soul is emotionally based, and emotions are like waves of the sea. Settling them can be difficult; they have a will of their own. While reading Psalm 51 you would have caught David's deep regret in sinning against God and the soul-searching cry of his heart!

And yet crying out with the pain of regret does not mean to say that consequences would not follow. Consequences follow the sinful acts we sanction, and in David's case that meant the child Bathsheba carried would die.

Yet David fell on his face, cried out to God for mercy, and pleaded for the life of his child. Let's read on...

2 Samuel 12

16 "David therefore besought God for the child; and David fasted, and went in, and lay all night upon the earth.

17 And the elders of his house arose, and went to him, to raise him up from the earth: but he would not, neither did he eat bread with them.

18 And it came to pass on the seventh day that the child died. And the servants of David feared to tell him that the child was dead: for they said, Behold, while the child was yet alive, we spake unto him, and he would not hearken unto our voice: how will he then vex himself, if we tell him that the child is dead?

19 But when David saw that his servants whispered David perceived that the child was dead: therefore David said unto his servants, is the child dead? And they said He is dead!"

"Not my will but Thy will be done" is a great place of submission. No matter how we feel, no matter what has taken place, or is yet to take place, one of the most important revelations in the Bible that we can live by is: "Not my will but Thy will be done!"

"But Jesus said unto them, ye know not what ye ask: can ye drink of the cup that I drink of? And be baptized with the baptism that I am baptized with?
And they said unto him, we can. And Jesus said unto them, ye shall indeed drink of the cup that I drink of; and with the baptism that I am baptized withal shall ye be baptized." Mark 10:38

What was Jesus saying? What cup were they to drink? What baptism would they be baptised with? Well, firstly, He was not talking about communion but about something called "the will of God".

The "cup" was the Cross that lay before Him, and the baptism was the path to that Cross that had been planned for Him before He came to this earth.

Have you ever thought about the fact that God loved you so much that He allowed you to be born! God looked down through eternity and sketched out the choices that would come across your path. He saw the decisions that you would make, including the wrong ones. God has seen them all and yet, knowing the mistakes you would make, He looked for someone who could restore you, no matter what you had done. Only His Son Jesus could be that person.

No matter where you are now, no matter what you have done, no matter that you are planning to come to the feet of the Master, Jesus knows exactly where you are and how to turn your life around for good!

It is on the journey of 'the way of the cup' you will realise a point comes that brings you to a 'baptism of death', where not thy will be done but His. We must choose to drink of this cup if we are to move into the glory realm of God, for flesh is not trusted and cannot stand in the glory realm.

Even the innocent Jesus would have to drink of the "cup" of God's will choosing to walk in the power of God in the path of God will take us to a place of choice – Will we drink of the cup?

David drank of it, and in so doing put his faith in the righteous judgement of God. Those who drink of it surrender themselves to the Father. Each going through the pain of losing something they held dear to find something greater in the Father.

Mark 14:36 – "*And he* (Jesus) *said, Abba, Father, all things are possible unto thee; take away this cup from me: nevertheless not what I will, but what thou wilt.*"

Chapter 17

Exposure to Another

Nakedness can be easy for some, but if at some point in life you have been abused, exposure of yourself can be terribly difficult. It can be uncomfortable to the point that you feel like you are peeling off your skin. Exposure after abuse can be too terrifying for words.

Just hearing the word "exposure" brings fear to some people. It takes them back to the day or night when their innocence was taken from them after the shadow of evil had fallen upon them. But if you are such a person, I would like you to begin thinking that whatever the devil did to try to destroy you, God can turn it around; and for this to happen I need you to understand that exposure in its proper setting is good.

Most of us would know the word 'exposure' means "to uncover, to reveal", but the dictionary definition of "exposure" can also mean "to bring to light".

Do you know that God likes to bring things to light? It may not be in the way you might think, and certainly not what the devil has led you to believe. It is the way God did with David, or the way He exposed my deep secrets. God brought them to Light not to destroy me, but rather so that He could get my attention long enough to change me, forever.

I want you to note that God never at any time exposed my secrets for someone else's scrutiny. He did so in a room where a prophet and I were alone. Please underline in your conscience (your moral consciousness) that God does not bring a life into disgrace. God has an enemy who is fully intent on doing that. Why then would God or someone who ministering in God's name do that? My friend, if someone is threatening you like this, you can be sure that their threat is not based on love but on fear; and that which is based on fear is not from God.

I am aware that there are times when as leaders we have to stand up and give an account of our actions, but where and how is up to us. Scripture says that we are to judge ourselves. It is not for me to judge you in the sight of others, or to publicly disgrace a person who has fallen. The Bible says:

Galatians 6:1 – "Brethren (and note that this does not refer to a sinner), if a man be overtaken in a fault (sin), ye which are spiritual, restore (complete thoroughly) such a one in the spirit of meekness; considering thyself, lest thou also be tempted (put to the test)."

1 Corinthians 13 v 4 Amplified Bible

"Love endures long and is patient and kind; love never is envious nor boils over with jealousy, is not boastful or vain glorious, does not display itself haughtily.

[5]It is not conceited (arrogant and inflated with pride); it is not rude (unmannerly) and does not act unbecomingly. Love (God's love in us) does not insist on its own rights or its own way, for it is not self-seeking; it is not touchy or fretful or resentful; it takes no account of the evil done to it [it pays no attention to a suffered wrong].

[6]It does not rejoice at injustice and unrighteousness, but rejoices when right and truth prevail.

[7]Love bears up under anything and everything that comes, is ever ready to believe the best of every person, its hopes are fadeless under all circumstances, and it endures everything [without weakening].

[8]Love never fails [never fades out or becomes obsolete or comes to an end]."

God wants you to know that He is LOVE! Not just that He has Love but that He IS Love. Everything God does is birthed in Love. God never intended that anyone on this earth who has ever lived, who is now living or who will live be birthed in any way other than in and through His Love. For many the most favourite verse in the Bible is one that they have heard so often they've become numb to it. It's John 3:16, of course. But before you switch off because you know it by heart, I want you to read it with added meaning; and as you do, let it penetrate your heart.

John 3:16

"For God so greatly loved and dearly prized YOU (world) that He [even] gave up His only begotten (unique) Son, so that (YOU) whoever believes in (trusts in, clings to, relies on) Him shall not perish (come to destruction, be lost) but have eternal (everlasting) life"

Can you see that before you were formed God made a way for you; that He chose the seed and the womb that would bring you forth upon this earth? You are not here by mistake because God makes no mistakes. You did not arrive on this earth by accident but by Divine Purpose. The Eternal God breathed upon your spirit while you were in the womb, and you became the very person God knew you would become. Your choices in life have not surprised God because He knew the paths that you would take. He knew that at this exact moment you would be reading this page. Nothing you have done or ever will do will surprise Him. I would ask you right now to lay your life afresh before Him. You have nothing at all to fear but everything to gain. You might say, "I have missed it! I am a minister but I'm not good enough!" You might say many things, but I want you to say just one thing: "Help me Jesus!" Nothing more, nothing less! But help me Jesus!

I used to think I had to sing so many hymns, clap so many times, pray for so long, hunger for days while fasting, but I was wrong.

There I was trying my best and you know what? Our best is not good enough. We can never repay the Master for what He has done for us! That's why God's gift to us is called GRACE. It is undeserved and cannot be earned.

I remember the first time God spoke audibly to me. Now you might say, "God does not speak audibly!" Did Adam know God from a book? No, Adam knew God because God actually spoke to him and they had conversations! God speaks and the Bible confirms to us that we are hearing from Him, because what He is saying is filtered and authorised by Scripture.

Imagine having a conversation with God, the person who knows the tomorrows of your life. Imagine knowing what is going to happen to you before it ever gets onto the path of your life. A conversation with a head of government would be a thing we would talk about for years, but has it ever occurred to you that God – the One who made the universe, has made an appointment in His diary to talk to you?

Have you ever realised that before Jesus was present in the womb of Mary, God had spoken about it to His people; and that after the resurrection of Jesus, God still spoke to His people? The Bible actually records it: God speaks to His people!

For me, fresh in the faith, devoted in all avenues, I pulled out my usual spiritual shopping list of goodies: things I wanted God to provide. On my knees beside my bed, I had been praising for a while and then went off on my spiritual shopping spree...

"Dear God, I pray for Sandra: that you would heal her! You know, Lord, that she does not deserve to be sick, and I bind the devil and I release spiritual blessings to be poured all over her. And as for Charlie, he really needs a new car! God, without one, how can he get to work? So I loose a new car into his life and I bless it!" On and on I went for several hours, and each day the list got longer. Was I a follower of Christ or what?

When I think back I can see how immature I was and how spiritual I thought I was! For instance, what does "spiritual blessings poured all over her" mean? Even to this day I don't know (which maybe is why I stopped praying it). As for "loose a car" does that mean that the car has been chained up some-where, or (worse still) that the car will somehow appear out of heaven? What if the guy can't afford the daily costs of running his new car? Plus the fact that a new car always needs to be bigger and better because, after all, that would only be increasing faith in action.

Previous to the time when I met the afore-mentioned lady in the mental institution, the one who was confessing but not understanding, I would have prayed somewhat the same, with the attitude that at least I was obeying God's word. Day and night I would kneel and pray for other's needs, for need after need. I'm sure that God must have thought I would make a great employee for a fast food restaurant, "Next please!"

It's funny in a way how you always remember the things that change your life. That day in prayer was going to be different, because it would totally change my understanding of God.

I had done my praising and was halfway through my spiritual grocery list. I think God was more laughing at me than ticking off the many things I was asking for. Right in the midst of one important sentence requesting God's answer to a very serious need, an audible voice spoke from behind me, saying, "Maurice!"

I was so into my rants and raves of making needs known to God that even though I heard it, I kept on speaking. Yet the voice had got my attention.

I continued to pray, while my mind divided itself into registering prayer needs and trying to figure out who owned this voice -- one I never had heard before. I was like a baby that hears its father speak but knows not that it's the father.

I kept on praying and after what seemed a couple of minutes I heard it again, a voice saying, "Maurice!"

This time, the voice not only got my attention but also got my back up! How dare someone come into my room and interrupt me while I am in prayer with God! Though still on my knees, I turned my head towards the bedroom door, a distance of two feet from me and saw that no one was there.

I was hearing a voice from behind me in my room, and yet there was no one in the room! My mind now began to take a beating.

Then a thought came to me: "Maybe it is the Holy Spirit!" You would never guess what I did next; in fact I don't believe anyone would guess what I did to God! I put my hands over my face and pretended to pray out loud while looking through the gaps between my fingers! One way or another, I was going to catch this person who was repeating my name! No one was going to make a fool of me! After all, wasn't I the spiritual one?

Then this awareness came upon me that someone or something was in the room near me, and with this awareness came a peace that seemed to fill the room. The words I was saying seem to slip away into the distance. Time seemed to stand still. Then it happened again, and this time I was waiting. Over my right shoulder, in my right ear, I heard the voice again: "Maurice!"

I was still on my knees and my heart swelled up with His love. In the way God found a stable in Bethlehem to birth His plan: that day in a small village in Northern Ireland, the God of the universe had come into a room that was even smaller than a stable, just to make Himself known to me.

For those who still find this hard to believe, think of what a hard pill it would be for children to swallow if their natural father watched over them but never ever spoke to them. I believe that the God of the heavens is far greater than a natural father and so I also believe that our supernatural Father wishes to hear how His children are and to know what they are doing. There is no sweeter moment in a storm than when you hear the voice of the Father, and the clearer His voice becomes the smaller the storm becomes.

Scripture tells us that God even knows you by name. In the Old Testament Moses heard his name called by God from out of a burning bush (Exodus 3:4). In the New Testament Saul (Apostle Paul) clearly heard Jesus call him by name (Acts 9:4).

Do you realise that God knows your very name? That day in my bedroom, as I heard the Master's voice calling me by name, I went from praying a spiritual grocery list to becoming a person whose prayer life had changed. I understood how to pray. It makes a difference when the Master reveals Himself to you!

In the midst of King David's 'storm' not only did His Father in Heaven speak to him through the prophet Nathan, but he also fulfilled that which He had spoken when David's child died. The cup that Jesus drank was the cup from which we all must drink. David drank from the cup, "Not my will but Thy will be done." After so doing, David arose to face the challenge of a new day in God.

2 Samuel 12

20 *"Then David arose from the earth, and washed, and anointed himself, and changed his apparel, and came into the house of the LORD, and worshipped: then he came to his own house; and when he required, they set bread before him, and he did eat.*

21 *Then said his servants unto him, what thing is this that thou hast done? Thou didst fast and weep for the child, while it was alive; but when the child was dead, thou didst rise and eat bread.*

22 *And he said, while the child was yet alive, I fasted and wept: for I said, who can tell whether GOD will be gracious to me, that the child may live?*

23 *But now he is dead, wherefore should I fast? Can I bring him back again? I shall go to him, but he shall not return to me."*

Are you ready to rise to the challenge of a new day in the service of God?

Chapter 18

When Your No Means Yes!

'No' is one of the smallest words in the English language, and yet if we would say "No" more often in life, we would see far better outcomes.

When I was introduced to the Christian world, everything seemed to be "Yes!" I was taught that it was improper to say "No!"

This took place to the degree that I would say "Yes" when I should have said "No". Such is the power of that little word it can actually force one to lie!!! Why is it? Why is it that we feel it is wrong to say No?

If we find it difficult to say 'No' then we will always say the opposite and we know what that word is – "Yes!" We become, a Yes-er (my word) everything is "Yes, Yes, Yes!"

When God challenged me on this area it brought such a freedom to me that I never realised how bound up I was. And do you know the reason why we do not have the freedom to say No? FEAR

FEAR is one of the greatest weapons that the enemy uses against God's people. I like what someone came up with one time. They said FEAR is **F**alse **E**vidence **A**ppearing **R**eal – that is brilliant.

Fear is the only thing that is stopping you from saying, "No!" When that image of a man or woman is flashed in front of you, learn to say "No!" When that secret meeting is being arranged, learn to say "No!" When that touch from the third party comes into play, learn to say NO!

The word 'No' was so far out of my language that even when I started to say 'No' people took it as a 'Yes!' Even when I had finished an impressive meal, being stuffed to the throat with food and my stomach crying out 'mercy' and they asked, "Do you want more?" I would say, "No!" They responded, "Oh, sure you want more" as they dished extra out, while my eyes were rolling around in the back of my head declaring that a heart attack was on the way! If we find it difficult to say No then we need to know why?

If you are one of those people who like flattery, then without a doubt you know what I am saying, that your No actually means Yes.

The object of your desire is approaching you and they make a move on you (You know what I mean) and for that split second you let your eyes meet theirs and then you pull away. They come near to you and create that chat line of which even though you are saying 'No' every other part of you is saying 'Yes!' And you know that your No's are actually Yes's but you are drawing them over a line – into your trap. Listen carefully, everything that we do is laid bare before God, every trap that we set, every deception that we have designed, every path of destruction that we lead someone down, it is all known and seen by God.

Whether it is the sexual path or the meal that causes heart-attacks we all must learn that our "No's must be a No as Scripture shows

James 5:12 The Message

"And since you know that he cares, let your language show it... Just say Yes or No"

I cannot emphasis how important 'No' is for you. We use excuses for not saying 'No.' If I say No that person will be offended, they will not understand. If the word of God in James 5:12 says we should use 'No' then it is good enough for me and should be for you – Remember our standard should be the Word of God.

Let's deal with saying No but still meaning Yes. When that third party is still flaunting themselves at you in that subtle way you will find that Samson's No's were Yes's. If you have had any form of sexual activity in your life then I think we have all been there. That touch, the heart getting faster, and you know that your 'No' has absolutely no power in it – the truth is 'No' being such a small word seems so difficult to say – maybe you need to learn to say 'No!"

If you are like I was in my past then you need to do what I had to do. I had to practise saying "No!" Can you believe that? Yes, it is true. When God showed how wrong I was in not being able to say 'No' as shared with you, even when I did say 'No' it never made any difference – people just seemed to carry on. Then I found it easy to blame them. I was like Adam, it was their fault but God reminded me, Maurice it is your fault, I have given you dominion, authority – learn to say NO!

I went into my bedroom and started to say 'No' to the mirror! I said, it low, I said it high, but one thing for sure, when I came out of that room my 'No' was a 'No!' And because of that the roads in life that I could have easily gone down, I never went down not because of spirituality, but because I learnt to say 'NO!'

Practise it now if you can, say No and say it at all different levels until the freedom inside hits you too. And remember if you can't say No, every time the phone rings you will answer, every time you sit to rest you will get up, every time that God allocated time for you and Him – you will not be able to make it. Saying 'No,' presents you with another choice that you did not have. I pray that 'No' will not be seen as a negative word but something very positive in all of our lives. And for those who have children teach them to say No at an early age it may just save their life!

Chapter 19

The Scripture Stylist

To everything there is a season...a time to be born and time to die... (Ecc. 3:1, 2)

Seasons are something that comes upon us whether we like it or not. Some people enjoy the winter for the snow, while others dread the snow coming. But one thing is for sure, winter is coming and if you are wise you'll prepare for it. Before there was gas, oil or electric heating in homes the people went out to the forests before the winter came and cut down trees and prepared the wood into logs. Winter was coming and they were not going to get caught out of supplies.

Then there are those whose attitude is, 'tomorrow I will do that'. You know what? Tomorrow never comes.

Seasons are only for a period of time, so the reason why winter and summer are called seasons is - they do not last forever.

You may have entered into a season of temptation where you have been tempted to have an affair away from your spouse, or even God. But I want you to know that temptation is only for a season and that season must end. You need to set the alarm clock of your mind to ring louder than ever before – the season is over, temptation is over and one must close the door.

Closing a door to anything is difficult, and closing a door to a relationship is one of the hardest things that one can ever do.

The Bible says, Matthew 6:24

No man can serve two masters: for either he will hate the one, and love the other; or else he will hold to the one, and despise the other...

If you are a Christian, then you're a Christian based on the Bible being true. But if you hold the right of being higher than God, and you take verses out to suit you then you are what I call a 'scissor picking Christian'. There are those who use Scripture to line up with the wrongs they do or believe in. They say this verse I agree with, but this verse I don't. They are what I would call 'Scripture Stylists.' Like a hairstylist they style hair to suit the person's looks. In like manner 'Scripture Stylists' style Scripture to suit what they believe.

The first time I ever encountered a 'Scripture Stylist' was on the first day I started my new office job. And you know how it is first day in the office, all eyes are on the new comer and those who deem you as a threat will at some point make themselves known to you.

Anyhow, days went by and, 'bang', the 'Scripture Stylist' took off with all the staff at his disposal, watching and listening as he asked me, "And what church do you go to?" New to the faith, I thought a Christian (in this case) asked this question more on the grounds that they were genuinely interested in me, but not so. The motive for asking me was to find out what I believed in compared to his doctrine! In other words, if I said that I went to such and such a church then he would simply conclude that he knew what I believed. Ignorantly, I told him and instantly his voice rose. And for the next thirty minutes he raged out, "So you believe this and that." Oh, he had his audience hooked to every word. I stood there like a lamb to the slaughter in front of these people. By now this guy's blood veins were raised in his neck. Such was his anger being unleashed and still I had said nothing. Then my eyes were drawn to a pair of scissors and a thought came. So I lifted the scissors, and, (no I wasn't going to kill him), holding the scissors I gently asked him, "Do you have you your Bible with you?" He said, "Yes!" I then said, "Give me your Bible," which he did. I opened it up to one of the portions he had mentioned and said to him, "so you don't believe in this part?" He said, "No!" I opened the scissors and pretended that I was going to cut out the portion. He shouted, "What are you doing to my Bible?" I looked at him and said, "Well, why carry all this weight around with you when you only need a certain amount. You only believe part of it anyway!" He snatched his Bible from me and knocked chairs over to get out of the office. But you know what - It was a 'Scripture Stylist' that left the office in a hurry that day because "Truth was revealed".

If we start to style Scripture to suit ourselves, it will lead us to a pathway of spiritual blindness, believing we can see, when in reality – we have been deceived. For we cannot serve Truth and Deception!

We either accept the Bible as Truth or we become a 'Scripture Stylist,' styling, cutting and twisting Scripture to make our soul and flesh content within the confines of a suitable doctrine.

Religion builds from the outward (exterior) but God builds from the heart (interior). From the day we come forth from our mother's womb we are trained to look at the exterior (the area we judge) not seeing it's the interior (what God judges) that we need to uncover.

Let us unfold this a little more...

"And when the woman saw that the tree was good for food, and that it was pleasant (to long for) to the eyes, and a tree to be desired (take pleasure in) to make one wise, she took of the fruit thereof, and did eat, and gave also unto her husband with her; and he did eat." Genesis 3:6

What drew them to consider the 'more' of what God had given them? The serpent led them to see only the exterior. They stepped from what God had for them – the interior to exterior – outside of God's will.

To step from what God has to what the devil has planned is rooted in deception. The serpent spoke in the garden and asked, "Hath God said?" (Gen. 3:1) Matthew records the devil sowing the same seed to Jesus but the results would be different...

Matthew 4:3

"And when the tempter came to him,(Jesus) he said, If thou be the Son of God, command that these stones be made bread.

4 *But he answered and said, It is written, Man shall not live by bread alone, but by every word that proceedeth out of the mouth of God.*

5 *Then the devil taketh him up into the holy city, and setteth him on a pinnacle of the temple,*

6 *And saith unto him, If thou be the Son of God, cast thyself down: for it is written, He shall give his angels charge concerning thee: and in their hands they shall bear thee up, lest at any time thou dash thy foot against a stone.*

7 *Jesus said unto him, It is written again, Thou shalt not tempt the Lord thy God.*

8 *Again, the devil taketh him up into an exceeding high mountain, and sheweth him all the kingdoms of the world, and the glory of them;*

[9]And saith unto him, All these things will I give thee, if thou wilt fall down and worship me.

[10]Then saith Jesus unto him, Get thee hence, Satan: for it is written, Thou shalt worship the Lord thy God, and him only shalt thou serve.

[11]Then the devil leaveth him..."

We could think that the devil quoted three random statements to Jesus. But if we think this then we do not realise just how tactical and cunning the devil is. Each one of those temptations was well thought out and designed to take Jesus from the interior of God's will of who He was, to the exterior - promising more. Each statement to Jesus was directed at the three gateways of the soul.

1 John 2:16

"For all that is in the world, the ***lust of the flesh****, and the* ***lust of the eyes****, and the* ***pride of life****, is not of the Father, but is of the world."*

Any one of the three - The lust of the flesh, the lust of the eyes and the pride of life will carry us, like the first man and woman, to a place outside of God's will. To focus on the exterior of what we see by our natural eyes will cause us to not see by our spiritual. For me, I was about to find out how the exterior drew me in.

The word "Attention" echoed through the hall that I had just entered (deafening any new comer) as the commander of the Boys Brigade was letting us know just who the boss was. Copying what everybody else was doing, we rallied into standing as straight as we could in a line, shoes gleaming with our little shorts on us. Yes, we were only children, but to the commander that did not matter – we had signed up!

Months earlier I had watched the Boys Brigade parading through our small village, and listened to the commander shouting, "Left right, left right." Gosh, how I thought it would be cool to be in that parade with them! From that moment on I sought to join the Boys Brigade! The problem was I had been drawn into the exterior and never realised what took place in the interior. You see it was thrilling to watch those boys marching to the beat of a drum, but no-one told me there was another side to it – the side of discipline – when the commander says, "jump," you – JUMP!!!

You see, I had signed up for the exterior but it didn't take me long to learn that for the exterior to present itself the way it should, a commander must work from the inside out. Likewise as followers of Christ, we signed up to represent Jesus. How much more then should we be willing to allow our Lord to correct the interior parts of our being in order for our exterior to display the Glory of His Majesty?

God is interested in the real you, not just the 'put on your best act' for meetings. When you allow Him to find the real you - God will build you from the foundation up.

When children come forth from the womb of their mother they are normally born with a set of ears for the purpose of helping them to hear what is going on in this natural world. And, when the Holy Spirit comes into our lives we become born-again. As His seed enters our spiritual womb a new creation springs to life bringing forth the character of Jesus Christ through us.

But as a child is born with ears to hear the natural sounds that surround it, are you aware that when your spiritual being is born it has also been given a set of ears?

Revelation 2:7 *"He that hath an **ear**, let him hear what the Spirit saith unto the churches"*

Why would your spiritual being have a set of ears except there be something to hear that the natural ears cannot hear! But what could it be?

Your spiritual ears are for one person only – to hear the voice of the Holy Spirit, for there is no other voice like it!

Focus on His voice. What is He saying to you? After all, if you are born-again you have been given a set of ears to hear what He is saying to you and how He is directing you.

When we live only through our natural ears the 'Blame Game' is never far away, "There she goes again, it's her fault, no it is his fault, and she said that, no he said that!" On and on it goes and really what are they saying? It is not my fault, it is always someone else's! My partner is not, will not, let me, show me, uses me, angers me, etc. Have you noticed the most common word used in that last sentence is ME?

It's that same thing that Adam did, he blamed everyone but himself – Are you there?

That root, which is based in the fall of man and the pride of man, must be cut off and our trust must be transferred from ourselves to God. He alone must be the author and finisher of our faith. (Heb. 12:2)

Your mind will play all types of tricks on you, pointing fingers at your partner, "It is their fault." But one thing I have learned, even though it may have taken me awhile, (some are slower than others) is that most of the mistakes that happened in my life are due to wrong choices I have made.

When I trace it back to where it first connected, most of the time the answer rings loud and clear – You made the wrong choice; you took the wrong information, you, you, you – the responsibility lies at your door.

King David could have blamed being tired in order to keep him from the frontline and at home that day. Or maybe it was Uriah. He was at war (even though David sent him) and he should have been at home with his wife. Or maybe it was Bathsheba - she was too beautiful. Excuses, excuses David could have used, but the real question is, when do we stop styling excuses and Scripture to suit what we do and take on TRUTH?

David threw himself at the feet of the Master and never blamed anyone but himself. And when he came to himself God came to Him. If you do the same, a miracle for your life is about to happen – The Promised Land is ready and God is waiting on you!

Chapter 20

Play is about to Begin

Each day we spend a lot of time talking to one another and saying things like, "Did you see..." or "Did you hear..." But have you ever thought of what we will talk about in eternity?

Could it be that when we get to heaven each of us will share with the saints our own personal story of stepping into the promises of God? Patriarchs like Abraham, sharing how God promised him a son through the barren womb of his wife Sarah. Peter telling of the day he found water to walk on at Jesus command. John sharing what it was like to be close enough to his Master to rest his head on his chest. Noah's story of how God told him to build an ark to escape a flood, when the word "rain" was not even in his understanding! All those and more penned testimonies of how they heard from God. Yes, we will all have a story to tell of how we walked with God and He with us in our lifetime. How will your story end?

We will have Eternity to share how we came to the realization that the only way we would see God move was to yield to Him completely. As the scripture says, *"Not by might nor by power but by My Spirit says the Lord!"* Zechariah 4:6

King David found himself in this situation. He had heard the promises of God, but now, after his fall, the promises of God seemed to have faded into the distance.

I am sure of two things: first that David and Bathsheba both knew they could never undo what they had done; and second, they decided from that day forward, God would come first in their lives.

After this fresh surrender of their lives to God, they heard another knock. The greatest coach that ever came upon this earth, the Holy Spirit, had just walked into the changing rooms of David and Bathsheba's hearts with a revelation, "Don't say that you have missed it, because in

Me nothing is ever missed. Get yourself ready; play is about to begin again; and in this part I will be your guide!" The knock this time would not bring them bad news but good news – news that they were forgiven!

Let's see what happens when God is allowed to enter the changing rooms of our hearts.

2 Samuel 12:24

"And David comforted Bathsheba his wife, and went in unto her, and lay with her: and she bare a son, and he called his name Solomon: and the LORD loved him."

Wow! Did you read that? David and Bathsheba had a son whom they named Solomon: "one who recompenses" – who compensates for that which has been lost.

David knew that having again put God first in their lives, good would be the final outcome. Scripture tells us that the Lord loved Solomon!

You must stop trying to do things in your own strength. You must come to the place where you accept that God has a call on your life. God is only waiting for one thing – your surrender to Him. It's time for you to make a full surrender!

Have you realised that, according to the story of David, you are entitled to a fourfold restoration from the Lord?

Let's read 2 Samuel 12

6 *"And he shall restore the lamb fourfold, because he did this thing, and because he had no pity."*

Remember this: God is not out to get you! He is not out to destroy your life! God is FOR YOU and you need to cement this into your life as a sure foundation stone. No matter what you are going through; God still wants the best for you!

This Scripture tells us that if a wrong has been done to you, then you have the right to receive a fourfold blessing. But what if you are the one who has done the wrong?

This may shock you, but whether you have done the wrong or have been the innocent victim of a wrong, the fourfold blessing is there to be attained! The reason is? We do not fight against flesh and blood but against evil spirits (Eph. 6:12). It is evil spirits that seek to destroy you; and whether in the circumstance you are innocent or not, it is a spirit that steals, kills and destroys (John 10:10). We are merely vessels of honour or dishonour (2 Tim. 2:20). This reveals that a spirit can pull someone's strings as though they were a puppet. Mark 9:21-22 gives us a clear understanding of this.

20 *"And they brought him to [Jesus]: and when he saw [Jesus], straightway the spirit tare him; and he fell on the ground, and wallowed foaming.*

21 *And he asked his father, how long ago is it since this came unto him? And he said, of a child.*

22 *And oftentimes **it** hath cast him into the fire, and into the waters, to destroy him: but if thou canst do anything, have compassion on us, and help us."*

Did you notice verse 22? "It hath cast him into the fire..." Something was pulling the child's strings! So Jesus took out His 'scissors' of authority and cut off every attachment that held this child to the spirit realm – Praise the Lord!

Based on this truth, David realised he was a pawn in the devil's hands and came with the brokenness of a surrendered heart to God. The law of the fourfold that had been used for shepherds (see end note) was now received by a king thus revealing God is no respecter of persons (Acts 10:34) to those who follow Him.

End Note

This law was mainly used in the case of shepherds whose sheep had been stolen. When the thief was caught, they had to restore to them the value of the sheep four times. Zacchaeus also mentions this law (Luke 19:8)

Chapter 21

Will I Stir or Not Stir?

With Irish weather being the way it is, especially in the winter, how we love homemade Irish Soup! Everything you could imagine is in our soup!

We know that the success of a good soup is not about stirring it or just leaving it to stew on the stove. No, to get the right texture in the soup, one must stir the soup then allow it to sit.

When you ask most young teenagers what they enjoy doing, they will say many different things. But I have never heard of one who enjoyed stirring soup. As a teenager I would watch my granny as she spent all morning prepping the carrots, onions, potatoes, ham, leeks, and just about everything you might imagine. Off they would go into a big saucepan! My job was to use the wooden spoon – and if I didn't, the wooden spoon would be used on me!

Gently I would stir the soup until I was told to stop. Then, a few minutes later, I would be told to start stirring the soup again, only to be told later to stop again. On and on it went to the point where I wanted to say – "Make up your mind – will I stir or not stir?" You see, I was missing the whole point of the exercise. The important thing to me was "make your mind up!" But the important thing to my granny was "texture and flavour" – getting both right.

As a child I never appreciated the quality of the soup my granny made, but it must have been very good, because people would purposely call into our home just to have a bowl of soup.

Do you know what I learned most from that? It was that she refused to let anything settle too long in that pot because it was the moving of it that helped release the full flavour of the ingredients. You may have allowed things in your relationship with your spouse to settle, and if that is so, I pray that within the next few hours and days God's large spoon will enter your marriage and begin to stir the ingredients of your love until its texture and flavour are as enjoyable to you as my granny's soup was to us.

Can God turn around a mistake you've made so that it works for your good? Yes, a hundred per cent YES! God can take that which seems a real mess and make it into something worth dancing about! Remember that a testimony only comes after a test; and for many of us love itself can be that test!

Love is like my granny's pot of soup; every so often we need to stir it up in us. Let me share with you the way mine got stirred...

Shortly after my wife and I were married, we had just sat down one night to dinner and "ding dong!" the doorbell rang. We had a visitor. I invited him in and my wife Maureen asked: "Would you like some dinner?" His reply was "Yes!"

The part I couldn't understand was where that dinner would come from, since I knew that Maureen had only just put all she had cooked on both our plates. Maureen just said, "Maurice will entertain you till I put your dinner out!" While I was chatting to our visitor my mind was occupied with the question: Where will Maureen get the extra dinner from? A few minutes passed and Maureen called us to the table. My mouth fell open! She'd had the audacity to reduce both our dinners by half and present it on another plate for you know who! I don't think I even tasted the food such was my indignation over what had taken place. I had been out working hard all day and had come home starving with hunger. Not only had I seen the dinner my wife had prepared for me -- I had actually sat down to eat it when the doorbell rang. Knowing that I deserved it only to watch another person eat it – well, that was something else! What made it worse was the visitor saying, "Hope you don't mind me eating this!" Before I could respond, Maureen said in her nice, kind voice, "No we don't mind!" How dare you say "we" I was thinking, when you never even discussed it with me!

You don't have to be too spiritual here to know that, after our visitor left, my wife looked me in the eye and asked "Is something wrong?" Fumes and smoke were coming out of my ears by this time, and so we had a marriage debate. She kept trying to tell me that it was only right that we should share. While all the time I was saying, "But it was mine, mine, mine I tell you!" Self was ruling me and didn't like being denied.

I have to say that it took several years for me to learn to be a giver. Many a time I sat thinking, go ahead -- choke on my dinner! Maybe a fright like that will teach you not to take food from my dinner plate! Then I might be able to pray for your healing! But no matter what I said, my wife refused to change in this matter; it seemed to me that she had never read, “Wives, submit to your husbands”! Even when I left her Bible open to where this Scripture was, she underlined it “Husbands, love your wives.” How could I win?

Who had the problem? Me! I didn’t understand that love involved giving and Maureen was a giver. Now, when I hear the front door bell ring, I eat as fast as I can! I’m joking! No, the difference now is that I seek to share, to give from what I have been given, even to the point of giving my dinner. The worst thing about it is that I now enjoy doing it. Husbands: listen to your wives!

Love is seen in that while we were yet sinners – some of us enjoying sinning; Christ died for us. The supreme example of love is Jesus Christ. There is no one like Him. He is all together wonderful.

When Love rules you put the needs of the other person before yourself.

Chapter 22

Restoration God's Style

As said earlier, the greatest weapon the devil has against you is FEAR. But do you remember I shared with you that it means: **F**alse **E**vidence **A**ppearing **R**eal. Fear is like a baby sucking on what we call a dummy but others call a soother or a comforter; but whatever you may call it you know that when a baby gets used to a dummy it doesn't like it when you try to remove it.

The thing that is wrong in a person's life, even in the case of an adulterous relationship - is like a soother (which a baby uses) that no one wants God to remove. But whatever the sin, He is saying 'If you let me take away that soother I will give you that which is right!'

The devil will tell you that there is nothing better than what you have. But I have to say, after studying the Scriptures, and as a result of my own walk with the Lord, God will always give you something better than what you have – and with Him you'll not need any soothers.

In discovering Christ as your Lord, you have won the greatest prize or gift that anyone can win! If God is for you, who or what can possibly be against you?

Whether you have been put out of a church or you are still in a church, never allow yourself to think like the prophet Elijah, who came to the point in life where he said to God, "I alone am left!" (1 Kings 19:10) God reminded him that He had reserved seven thousand who had not bowed their knees to Baal (1 Kings 19:18). But if Elijah had not won through to victory, the echo of God's voice would have rung out down through the years. It would have asked, "Who will stand up and be counted? Who will believe?"

I had been in a relationship with a girl for several years, and was hearing the sound of wedding bells when I came back to God, only to be told by Him, "Let go of her!"

My thoughts were scrambled! There came to my mind the happy times we'd had together, the furniture we had gathered for marriage, the strong emotional ties that bound us... I had even had her name tattooed on my arm. Yet God was saying, "Let go of her!"

You see, I had made a covenant with God when I came back to Him, and I knew that if my walk with Him was to continue, then I had to commit totally and without any reserve whatsoever to do whatever He asked of me. I had no idea that He was about to take me at my word.

For several weeks I fought God, but then began to notice that my life in Him was beginning to dry up, that my prayers were just words and my desire a mere habit, but God kept saying, "Let go!"

Nights usually brought dreams of the both of us together. Many were the times when my soul created its own counsel as to why I should not give her up. Truthfully, it was not easy to give up someone I so much desired, and yet I knew that if I were to become His servant, I had to obey the Master's voice.

The night before our separation God gave me a vision of her climbing a dark mountain and the sun coming up over the mountain and shining directly on her. Her face was bright, her clothes blew in the wind, and her hair was curly. Wait. Did I say "curly"? Yet never in all of her life had her hair been curly; and that made me wonder…

The next day we separated and ended our engagement. Peace settled into my spirit but my soul staggered all over the place - the comfort of the soother was gone.

Many a time I got into the car and, as had been usual, my hand would go out to hold hers. But no longer was her hand there. Tears would come and my soul would cry out. Pictures of her would flash in my mind. I had to remain true to the inner (interior) conviction that I was being obedient to God.

The devil would whisper in my ear that he would kill her, that God would never fulfil His promise of reaching her; but I decided that no matter how difficult life would be – and it was, I would go all the way with God.

Six months passed, and I was told that she was nearly killed in a car crash, but -- Praise the Lord – God had protected her from the death plan devised by the enemy!

Twelve months later I was asked to go to a meeting, but the night before going to that meeting, God woke me and told me to ask my ex-girlfriend to go with me. I phoned her and she agreed to go with me to the meeting.

When she came into the meeting that night I nearly fell off the seat! Was it her beauty, you ask? Was it the dress she was wearing? No, it was that her hair was now curly in the exact image and style I had seen in the vision! God had shown me a picture of the future, and the future had now become the present.

The preacher finished and began ministering to those with needs. But towards the end of the meeting he called out the ex-girlfriend and told her that God had a plan for her, and that tonight was her night to meet Him. That night she surrendered her life to the Lord, and as I watched her say the sinner's prayer her face shone as if the largest flash-lamp in the world had just switched on inside her head. The vision God had given me months earlier was happening right in front of my eyes! God had fulfilled His promise to me that He would give her the chance to know Him.

You may think I am now about to tell you that we got back together and lived happily ever after – isn't that the way fairy tales end? No, it was never His plan that we would get back together. It was just God fulfilling a promise. You see, when God asked to give her up, I said: "I have one condition: that you would give her the chance to come to know you!" And when God fulfilled that it released me to walk in the path He had planned for me.

You may ask, "Why would God not allow you to be with her rather than waste the years we had together?"

Remember what I have told you throughout this book: God knows the 'tomorrows' of your life. He knows exactly what it will take to make you into that person He has created you to be.

After I surrendered the ex-girlfriend to God, the devil many times brought to me the thought that I would never get anyone better than her; and there were times when I wondered if he might be right.

However, God does not lie, and years later I married my wife Maureen, of whom I cannot speak highly enough. She is my friend, my soul mate, lover, and a woman who hears from God as well. There were a number of times when I thought I was pretty sharp in some things, only to find out that her words led me more to the Master. The understanding of love she carries is second to none, as is also her loyalty and companionship. When her arms are around me the world becomes so small and her touch is such a comfort that being with her is restoration, God's style!

Many teach that God's restoration is based on the same idea as Man's. For example, if I lose ten coins then God will give me ten coins. But that is not God's, but man's idea of restoration.

Scripture says in Isaiah 55:8

"For my (God's) thoughts are not your thoughts, neither are your ways my (God's) ways, saith the LORD."

"God's ways are not our ways" tells us that we have to set aside our natural understanding to receive God's understanding; otherwise our mind will get in the way and we will never understand.

When David's son died, restoration from Man's point of view at the time would have been the son coming back to life. But God operates on a higher level than our natural thinking.

1 Corinthians 2:14

"But the natural man receiveth not the things of the Spirit of God: for they are foolishness unto him: neither can he know them, because they are spiritually discerned."

Here I use money as an illustration, but it could be anything. The thing to cement in your mind is that, in God's eyes, restoration is not you losing ten coins and God then giving you back ten coins. No, no, no! When you lose something; or rather, when the devil has stolen it; then you must know that God restores and gives back to you more than you ever lost. If I have lost ten coins then the minimum that God will return to me is eleven coins; not just ten. This is because He is the God of the overflowing cup, and so in restoring He will give back to you more than you ever lost.

Do you remember the story of Job? He lost everything: his children, his servants, his flocks – all of them stolen by the devil in disaster after disaster. Did he get his children back? Did he get his servants and flocks back? No! Did he experience restoration? Yes! Job went on to become the richest man in the world, with twice the number of flocks, servants and children.

When Jesus asked His disciples "Give me a boat to preach from," they did so and ended up needing more than one boat to bring home their huge catch of fish.

God sowed a Son into this world to the degree that His Son laid down His life. Did God reap one son back after His Son died? No, He sowed One Son and reaped millions of sons, not forgetting daughters, of course!

Everything about God's nature and character speaks to us of restoration, and His restoration is always better than Man's restoration.

Whenever God asks you to give something up, listen carefully! He is asking you to give it up because He has in mind something so much better for you! If the devil has stolen your ministry, partner, child, job or whatever else; or if he has led you astray from God, then know that "better" is on the way to meet you, if you are willing to get back on the right path, which is God's will for your life.

King David's child died, but God gave him another child called Solomon who became the wisest man who ever lived. Now, you may say there is no guarantee that God will give you another child. However, I can assure you that He will bring you to a place of understanding about your loss, and it will bring closure to the emptiness that's in your life. One thing you can know without doubt is that if you have anything wrong in your life to give over to God, then commit it to Him now, because when you do God will commit Himself to you! You will see a restoration greater than you could have ever imagined! In fact, I can honestly say that in the days and years to come, you will say, "I wish I had given it over to God sooner!" Never be scared to let go of that which is wrong in your life, because God has something greater for you. This is Restoration, God's Style!

Chapter 23

What's that I hear?

What if the Adulterous Spirit has so entwined itself with the Church that the Church does not recognise it? Could it be possible that the Church is in a backslidden state without knowing it?

Do you remember my definition of Adultery? It is when a third party comes into a relationship that is designed for two!

When you are "born again" there begins a relationship between God and you – TWO! Anything else that seeks to enter is Third Party involvement, which we know to be spiritual adultery!

Have you read the story of the Prodigal Son? It can be found in Luke, chapter 15.

11 "*And he said, A certain man had two sons:*

12 *And the younger of them said to his father, Father, give me the portion of goods that falleth to me. And he divided unto them his living.*

13 *And not many days after, the younger son gathered all together, and took his journey into a far country, and there wasted his substance with riotous living.*

14 *And when he had spent all, there arose a mighty famine in that land; and he began to be in want.*

15 *And he went and joined himself to a citizen of that country; and he sent him into his fields to feed swine.*

16 *And he would fain have filled his belly with the husks that the swine did eat: and no man gave unto him.*

17 *And when he came to himself, he said, How many hired servants of my father have bread enough and to spare, and I perish with hunger!"*

This story is not a parable -- an earthly story with a heavenly meaning

– it is a true story, one that actually happened. We know this because in verse 11 the Bible says, "A certain man had two sons."

The Law of Moses tells us that this son would have received one third of the value of his father's estate (Deut. 21:17).

The prodigal son went away on his journey into a far-off land, and in a time of famine joined himself to a citizen of that country. The stranger that he joined in the foreign country was so good a leader that he led the prodigal son to his swine-sty, where he was so hungry that he lusted for the very food the pigs ate. The prodigal son would never before have had anything to do with pigs – doing so was against his clean food principles. Now here he was in the company of swine and wishing he could eat their food!

Have you been on a journey like this? You have had the calling of God on your life and along with that have had a desire to walk daily with the Master. But now you find yourself doing things that you once said you would never do? Have you joined yourself to a party that has taken you so low that if someone were to come without warning into that room or that secret place you would be very embarrassed? These are signs that you are walking on a path that's taken you away from the Father.

I want you to take particular note of that part of verse seventeen, where it says "he came to himself" (to his senses).

I know of believers who are waiting for "the great falling away" the Bible teaches. Depending on your eschatology (your end-time doctrines), once this great falling away has taken place we are very close to getting out of here! The believers I mention wait to hear that droves of people are leaving the churches, because at some point they will in their natural wisdom pronounce, "It's the Great Falling Away!" Hopefully by now you have grasped that the devil deceives in the same way today as he did in the Garden of Eden. But deception can cover up something else that's taking place. This means that in our natural mind we may have formed a concept of what the Great Falling Away will be. But what if the Great Falling Away either is already happening or has happened already, right before the eyes of the Church, but we have not seen it? What if the churches were right now experiencing this Great Falling Away?

Religion is like the carrot hung in front of the donkey, in that it constantly keeps you moving forward but what you can see never satisfies you. When Jesus stood in front of those who were religious they did not recognise Him – the One they preached about in their gatherings was a stranger to them. It is any wonder then that Revelation says, "Behold I stand at the door and knock!" On whose door is Jesus knocking? It was the door of a church! Could it be that although we are "having church" we are not allowing Jesus to enter?

Revelation 3:20

"Behold, I stand at the door, and knock: if any man hear my voice, and open the door, I will come in to him, and will sup with him, and he with me."

This verse was not written to the sinner but to the Church -- the church at Laodicea (Revelation 3:14).

Could it be that the falling away is happening or even that it has happened?

When God directed me to read the prodigal son, He then asked me a question? At what point did the son backslide?

I knew God was not asking me the question because He didn't know why! He was asking me so I would look into it more deeply than I had. You see, I had been taught in various churches that the son was backslidden at the point when he ate the pigs' food, so I would have said the same. But my understanding of God's ways had taught me to look more deeply for the answer to His question. He knew what I had been taught. So, I concluded that the answer must be deeper, and then it came.

The son's backsliding did not begin at the end of his downward path when he reached the pigsty; his backsliding began in the moment he decided that he could do without a relationship with his father!

We are not backslidden because we are not in church, as many would teach. No, my friend, I have met many that are not in 'church' but are 'the Church'. By this I am referring to 'church' with a small 'c' as the building that people call church. Yet they can be in the building but still not in the Church. The Bible says that the gates of hell shall not prevail against His Church – that is not referring to brick and cement buildings but to people, to the people that are the Church with the BIG 'C.' Yes, as this story unfolds you will see that although people have thought that because you left a church you are backslidden that is not the case! Backsliding is not a condition that results from leaving a church, but rather one that results when we leave the Father's will, the plan that He has for your life. The moment the prodigal son left the Father he left the relationship and protection of his Father, and from then on was on the way down. He only realised that he had backslidden when he tried to eat pig food. What food will you try to eat before you come to yourself and make the decision to get out of where you are and get back again into the arms of your Father?

Let's take up the story again…

18 "I will arise and go to my father, and will say unto him, Father; I have sinned against heaven, and before thee,

19 And am no more worthy to be called thy son: make me as one of thy hired servants."

After we have fallen into sin we have a tendency to wait for an appointed moment when our relationship with the Father will be fully renewed. The prodigal son begins to retrace his steps to the point where he departed from his father. While on his way along the path of restoration we have previously mentioned, the son's mind slipped into fifth gear. He said, "I will be one of his hired servants. I can never again be his son because I am unworthy of that relationship." On and on the son walks, and all the time his mind is creating a picture. What I like about this son is that no matter what his mind told him, he retained his decision to again step over the threshold of his father's doorstep. He was nervous but determined.

20 "And he arose, and came to his father. But when he was yet a great way off, his father saw him, and had compassion, and ran, and fell on his neck, and kissed him.

21 And the son said unto him, Father, I have sinned against heaven, and in thy sight, and am no more worthy to be called thy son."

Do you see that? While he was a great way off! That does not mean that he was three or four feet away from him or a stone's throw – distance was involved! But in the Spirit there is no distance and I believe that when the son made that inner decision to arise and go the father's heart, he felt a tug that told him, My son is on his way home!

Did you notice what drove the father to the son when he saw him? It was compassion: the father had a heart for his wayward son.

While the son was yet a great way off, the father put on his running shoes and off he went, past his servants, past the doorkeeper, past the shepherds -- and he kept on running! The day the father had been waiting for had now arrived, and the father was not about to allow anything to hold him back!

I don't know about you but if you've ever worked with pigs you will know that they have their own unique smell -- and it is not the kind of fragrance you would wear to a party. To put it bluntly, they stink! When you go into the pigsty you try to keep your mouth closed. But you have to breathe, and so in a split second you take the smallest breath you can because of the foul smell. You may have entered that pigsty wearing the most expensive suit in town, but you will leave it smelling like a PIG!

Imagine this son who has not only been living with the pigs but eating their food. He doesn't smell anything like nice – just the opposite, because due to the hot climate the smell would have been worse than you can imagine.

But no matter what the son had done, no matter what he looked like (which I am sure was quite rough), no matter what he smelled like (which was like a pig), the father, listen carefully, the father, not one of the shepherds, not one of the hired servants, but the father threw his arms around him and kissed him! What a picture of the Father we serve, one who for every step we take towards him will take ten steps at a faster speed towards us. No matter what we have done or are doing, no matter what we look like, no matter how smelly we are, nothing, and I mean nothing, will stop Him 'running' to you once you decide to step towards Him again. Take that step towards Him, He's putting on His 'running shoes' and the one He is looking towards is YOU. Turn around and start walking back to Him!

22 *"But the father said to his servants, bring forth the best robe, and put it on him; and put a ring on his hand, and shoes on his feet:*

23 *And bring hither the fatted calf, and kill it; and let us eat, and be merry:*

24 *For this, my son was dead, and is alive again; he was lost, and is found. And they began to be merry."*

Have you ever been "dressed to kill" as the old James Bond movie put it? Clothes designer labelled and tailored so very up-to-date? I have not, but just think for a moment what it would be like. It would be nice!

This son came home dressed in dirty rags and the father ordered the servants: "Bring forth the robe that we were going to give to the charity shop!" No, he did not say that. Neither does our Father hold back from you anything that is good for you! He says, "Bring forth the BEST robe!" Remember the story of Joseph and his coat? Coats speak of relationship. As they entered into the house the father put a coat on him and said, "This is my boy!" The father was proud of him! Then a servant brought out an expensive ring. Taking up the ring, the father placed it on the son's finger. This was a declaration that the son now had the authority of his father; that the son's words would be as the father's words. But wait, still the father was not finished with the son – still something was missing: shoes! "Bring forth shoes and put them on him." Never again was he to go without shoes. At this point I am sure the son would have cried. It was hard enough to hear the father publicly declare that you were his son and to clothe you with his robe. As for giving you authority, well, that was something else! But to be given shoes to wear – well "blow me over!" as we say in Ireland.

You might be wondering what significance there is in the father giving him shoes. It signifies that not only did the father bring the son into a renewed relationship and give him his authority; it also means that he soothed the pain of his son's past by placing shoes on his feet. You see, in those days when a person was caught in a trap, his shoes were removed to hinder him from escaping. But this father, who was as full of love for his son as your heavenly Father is for you, said, "Put shoes on his feet." His son was to forget his painful past and know that he had a future to walk in. And what that father did for his son your Father will do for you!

What can we hear in the whisper of God's heart from heaven? It is "Restoration" – and that Restoration is coming your way!

Naturally speaking, the son had been wonderfully restored, but my hope is that you have come to see through what I have shared with you that God's restoration is always greater than Man's. The son's father looked across the yard and saw their prize possession, the fatted calf, the lot-fed one that was well looked after and pampered to the highest degree; and the father said, "Kill it and let us eat and be merry!" The cup of your Father in heaven is ready to be poured out; it is overflowing with love as He yearns for your soon return!

Chapter 24

The Chapter Not Written

I had been led to believe that George was an old miser. When I visited him I found that the few pieces of burning turf on his fire gave out just enough heat to remove the winter's chill from the room but not enough to warm it. George always wore a shiny suit. Not shiny in the expensive sense but shiny because he had worn it a hundred times too often. It was so shiny it seemed as if he polished it. George had lived a long life and had plenty of possessions: acres of land, bank accounts galore, the small house he lived in, and one that I didn't know about, his fancy house.

Although I had known George for many years, I had never known that he had a fancy house until he said to me one day, "Come, Maurice, let me show you something." We drove up a long lane until in front of us there appeared what looked like a new house. I was amazed at its grandeur, and wondered who lived in it and what George had to do with it.

These thoughts were running through my mind as George took a set of keys from his pocket, unlocked the front door, and led me inside. The house was finished to the highest standard. A large range (family cooker) was displayed in all its glory in the kitchen, where a table and chairs that looked unused sat in the middle of the room. Over the next thirty minutes he led me through the house, describing the features of its many rooms and letting me know how proud he was of it all. Me being me, I just had to ask George the all-important question: "Why are you sitting in an old house when you own this empty fancy house?" He took me back to the kitchen, pulled out a chair from the table, and said, "Take a seat and I'll tell you."

Struggling to sit comfortably on the chair due to his advanced age and poor health, George began to tell me the story...

"When I was your age, Maurice, I met this woman. She was lovely and for me there was nothing else in this life that I wanted, only her. Our friendship developed into a relationship and we decided that in a few years we would get married. But before that I would work day and night so that I could build her a house that she would be proud of. I had some money already set aside for a house, so we began to build this house, the one in which you are now sitting. No one knows the sweat and the pain that I went through during those years, as I laboured to finish the house and pay for it. Then came the time when the excitement of the marriage ceremony was only a few months away, and everything was on time."

George then interrupted his story by asking, "Maurice, what you think of the kitchen?" I said, "Great!" Then he asked, "Do you think this is a good house?" I said, "Sure, I think it is a brilliant house!" Tears appeared in his eyes as he asked, "What about the furniture and the décor: do you like it?" I said, "Yes I do, who chose it?" He said "My wife chose it all; whatever she requested I got for her!" He pulled open a drawer and lifted out some photos of their wedding day as he continued his story.

"The wedding was great. I could not have asked for a better day, and after our wedding ceremony and exchange of vows we went to the local hotel for the celebration and dinner. I will never forget that day!"

"After the celebration, my wife and I left the guests and drove off; in fact we were on our way to this very house, the home that I had built for her. On the way here, as we were about to pass her parent's home, she asked me to stop, as she had to do something. We stopped and she went into her parent's home while I sat in the car and waited for her to come out."

"Thirty minutes passed by, an hour passed by…and still no sign of her. Just as I was approaching the front door to find out why, her parents arrived back home from the wedding celebration. I told them what had happened and they said that they would go inside and see what if anything was wrong."

"The father came out to me after some time, and I knew by the look on his face that something was not right. He told me that my wife of several hours had locked herself in her bedroom and would not come out. He said, 'I would ask that you go home now to your house and come back tomorrow.'"

"Even though I was confused about what had happened the night before, I was up early the next day, freshly shaved and smelling good. Shortly after breakfast I arrived back at the home of my wife's parents. On the way to the front door I was met again by her father, and knew immediately that the day was likely not going to be a good one. Her father told me that his daughter had never wanted to get married, and that his point of view was that he had to stand by his daughter. I left their home that day a shattered man."

"That afternoon, Maurice, I came back to the house we are now sitting in and removed all my clothing and personal effects. What you are now seeing is the way everything was the day after my marriage, how I left it on that day nearly sixty years ago. You see, Maurice, I decided to wait for her. I was so determined that we would be together again that I have waited for her ever since."

"Waiting has been hard, but for sixty years I have longed for her to walk through the door of our home; but now, after all this time, I know that she will not be coming."

I asked, "What makes you think that after all this time she is not coming?" He said, "Last year, I walked behind her coffin and laid her to rest."

I was numb. What a sad story. What patience George had shown in waiting so long for the one he loved!

George staggered as he rose from the chair and reached for his walking stick. Gathering up the wedding photos, he placed them back in the drawer. He said, "Time to go home Maurice!" We left that fancy house and went back to the old house where he lived, back into that cold room where the pieces of turf in the fireplace were now burnt out. Yet somehow during the short time since I had left it, this small, cold room had taken on a new meaning. Gone was the image that had been portrayed to me of a miserly old man who had bought up many acres of land over the years just to make himself a name – it just wasn't so. Since that wedding day so long ago he had lived the fantasy that someday the wife he loved so much would walk in through the door, and that they would take up where they had left off. But, sadly for George, it was a long chapter in his life that would never be written.

Imagine how you would feel if, after turning to this chapter and reading its title: "The Chapter Not Written", you found yourself flicking through several empty pages. After some confusion you would have to skip to the remaining chapters. If you were from Ireland you would exclaim; "This author is nuts!" I'm sure we'd all think much the same. What a waste of paper! Why leave the pages empty when something could have been printed on them? I mean, after paying for the book you would expect something to be printed on every page!

What if I were to say that many lives are much the same; that many people find themselves either looking at or actually living blank lives. What if you were to find yourself living in the fantasy of hoping that somehow a particular person or thing you've long dreamed about would one day walk through your door and into your life? What if you were to read this chapter and realise that it reflected something that happened in your own life, and that since that time you have lived in the coldness of an empty life? What if in years to come you were able to follow after the coffin of your dream and watch as it is buried, all the time thinking about what could have been?

You look back through all the years that could have been different. You see how hard you worked and how long you waited for the dream that became no more than a fantasy. Hurt and pain can take you through several years of pain, but there comes a time when, before you know it, the old hand begins to shake, a walking frame is a welcome support, and the cake is unable to hold the number of birthday candles that represent the years you have lived.

My friend, we can all look back and think about what might have been, but looking back on life's yesterdays while time carries your body into life's tomorrows is a deception of the highest degree. Today will never come again. Never again will you breathe the same breath. A new day awaits you and a new breath is required!

The time has now come for us to deal with "What if?"

Chapter 25

What If?

You have just read the story of George, whose wife suddenly and unexpectedly decided not to spend her life with him. Many of you will be thinking, 'What if?' What if she had never gone back to her parent's house that evening? What if she had decided that her life with George was best for her? What if the newly married couple had spent the rest of their lives happily together?

Could there be a 'What if' in your life?

'What if' my skin colour was different? 'What if' I had studied harder? 'What if' I were taller or slimmer? 'What if'?

'What if' I had stayed with my partner? 'What if' I had married someone else instead? 'What if' I had not become involved in that affair? 'What if'?

'What if' I had never backslidden? 'What if' the adultery in my heart had not overwhelmed me? 'What if' I have allowed myself to be deceived into thinking that God was finished with me? 'What if'?

Questions, questions and more questions, all to the same beat – 'What if'? Every question echoing the same answer: You will never know.

You never know because every 'What if' is based on a fantasy, and you know that fantasy is defined as "the forming of unreal mental images". In many cases 'What if' should be filed under 'Deception'.

For instance: How many times have you thought of a previous partner and remembered those times together, and then fantasised about what they would be like now, the cuddle, the kiss, the... you tell me!

Lust has but one purpose, and that is to destroy the soul. Likewise, the act of fantasy has but one purpose, and that is to steal. You may ask, "Steal what?" Fantasy steals time that can never be repeated.

If you continue to fantasize, before you know it you will become like George, who continued to live a life that was over hours after it began, a life that existed thereafter only in his mind. Does this describe you?

The devil whispers in your ear: 'What if'? You feel that gentle touch, see that secret smile, and that you can have sex on the side? 'What if' you were to go down this easy path of pleasure and walk away from the path God has chosen for you? 'What if?'

How many times have I heard 'What if' in my ear! None of us is exempt from a 'What if' that points like a signpost to another, tempting life. The thought comes: What if I was to take that road?

That signpost competes with the road you are on for your attention, and can cause you to pause just long enough to gaze at it and wonder: 'What if?'

Let's go to a Bible story and see how one 'What if' worked.

In Genesis 19 we read the story of Abraham's nephew Lot, who lived with his family in the city of Sodom. God was about to destroy the city, so He sent two angels to Lot's home to bring him and his family out.

15 "*And when the morning arose, then the angels hastened Lot, saying, Arise take thy wife, and thy two daughters, which are here; lest thou be consumed in the iniquity of the city.*

16 *And while he lingered, the men laid hold upon his hand and upon the hand of his wife, and upon the hand of his two daughters; the LORD being merciful unto him: and they brought him forth, and set him without the city.*

17 *And it came to pass, when they had brought them forth abroad, that he said, Escape for thy life; look not behind thee, neither stay thou in all the plain; escape to the mountain, lest thou be consumed.*

18 *And Lot said unto them, Oh, not so, my LORD:*

19 *Behold now, thy servant hath found grace in thy sight, and thou hast magnified thy mercy, which thou hast showed unto me in saving my life; and I cannot escape to the mountain, lest some evil take me, and I die:*

20 *Behold now, this city is near to flee unto, and it is a little one: Oh, let me escape thither, (is it not a little one?) and my soul shall live.*

21 *And he said unto him, See, I have accepted thee concerning this thing also, that I will not overthrow this city, for the which thou hast spoken.*

22 *Haste thee, escape thither; for I cannot do anything till thou become thither. Therefore the name of the city was called Zoar.*

23 *The sun was risen upon the earth when Lot entered into Zoar.*

24 *Then the LORD rained upon Sodom and upon Gomorrah brimstone and fire from the LORD out of heaven;*

25 *And he overthrew those cities, and all the plain, and all the inhabitants of the cities, and that which grew upon the ground.*

26 *But his wife looked back from behind him, and she became a pillar of salt."*

You can see by reading this story that it was God's will for Lot and his wife and children to escape the city and not be consumed (v 15). If it had been God's will for them to perish along with everyone else, then God would not have sent His angels to rescue them. Do you remember reading earlier that a messenger in Bible days was someone on a mission, and that each mission had a goal. The angel's mission was to deliver Lot and his family from the doomed city.

During the family's escape from Sodom the angel gave them a warning (v 17): "... *Escape for thy life; look not behind thee, neither stay thou in all the plain; escape to the mountain, lest thou be consumed!"*

These directions were clear enough. Who could miss the meaning of "Look not behind"? But 'What if' -- those two small words that lead us to think that we are exempt from the consequences of our actions came into the mind of Lot's wife. 'What if I take a look behind? Just a quick glimpse! Lot will never know!' Surrendering to the thought of 'What if' she turned around and looked. When she did she was encased in salt and would remain stuck in the same place -- forever looking back and never able to go on. Are you like that? George was like that. Looking back at 'what if' he remained stuck in a fantasy that did not allow him to go on into a new day!

Can you hear the clock of time ticking, "Tick, tick, tick"? The clock of old age is also ticking and the grave is calling and warning you that time is running out... The question is: will you listen?

We all have taken knocks and bruises in life, and I'm sure that you've had your share - maybe more than your share. But I believe that you can rise above those hurts; that you can throw away the worn-out clothing that is so much like George's shiny suit, and be dressed again in the garments of righteousness!

God's will for you is wholeness in this life and a relationship with God and other people that is so special that Job describes it as: *"One is so near to another that no air can come between them."* (Job 41:16)

"No air can come between them" is what I would call a close relationship!

God desires the same for you! He desires that your relationship with Him be one of wholeness, and wants you to know that even from a fallen state you can be restored. This is Restoration God's Style!

Take a moment to follow the response of your heart and surrender yourself afresh to the Master. Lay yourself before Him from this day on with all your fears and doubts. The One who stilled the stormy waters will still your stormy heart.

Yes, I am sure that when you do, some will cross over to the other side of the street to avoid you, or frown at you and not speak to you. We will speak about them in the next chapter. But know this: once you ask the Lord for His forgiveness you will walk the path that King David walked, the path the prodigal son walked, the same path walked by all who have repented. It is a path of wholeness in a life walked by those who lives are fully surrendered to the King.

Philippians 1:6

"Being confident of this very thing, that he which hath begun a good work in YOU will perform it until the day of Jesus Christ."

Chapter 26

Watch out, there's a brother about!

When I came back to the Lord in my twenties, I thought that church people would be happy that this boy who knew how to sin had turned his back on it! The mates I had hung out with were the sort that would have laid down their lives for you. If I had phoned them at 3.00 am in the morning, they would soon have been at my door, no questions asked! My basic understanding of Christianity was that if those who are in the world are like that, then surely those in the Church must be better. But I was in for a shock!

I have given much thought to how I would bring you this chapter; how I could make the impact easier for you. A father would much rather be in pain himself than see his child in pain.

However I know of no other way then to tell you straight. Are you ready? Best if you sit down if you can. Here goes...

When you turn to Christ for a new baptism in His Love, not everyone will want to come to your glory party! You will need to do what I have done many times, and that is to rejoice in the Lord, with or without the music!

Could this be why the Bible never states that we should wait for people before rejoicing in the Lord? You must learn to celebrate alone in the presence of God. The good news is that when you do, no one will be there to spoil your party!

My saying that not all will celebrate your spiritual homecoming may come as a shock to you. However, as with other statements I have made, I will back them up with Scripture. Let's go back and finish the story of the prodigal son, which we began earlier.

[25] *"Now his elder son was in the field: and as he came and drew nigh to the house, he heard music and dancing.*

[26] *And he called one of the servants, and asked what these things meant.*

[27] *And he said unto him, Thy brother is come; and thy father hath killed the fatted calf, because he hath received him safe and sound.*

[28] *And he was angry, and would not go in..."*

I want you to take particular notice of the beginning of verse 28: "And he was angry, and would not go in..."

The "he" mentioned here was also a son of the father. The Bible states this quite clearly. And yet this son, even while living under the father's roof, still lived in his own will! We know this because envy rose up within him and he refused to go into the party. After all, the fatted calf had not been killed for him, had it?

Is this a picture of the state of the Church as most Christians know it? Do we have to go outside the walls of the Church to find the real Church because of the attitudes of churchgoers who have not yet surrendered their will? God wants us to be broken but not destroyed. Are we friends of God or servants of God?

Let me explain as I go deeper with this...

In Bible days there was a BIG difference between being someone's friend and someone's servant. The servant was employed to meet the needs of the employer. Whatever needed doing the servant did it – he served. He was known as "a hired servant". The maximum length of time an employer could keep a hired servant was six years. During that time the servant would learn his master's ways.

The Law of Moses stated that after six years of serving the servant was to be allowed to go free. For the master to obey the Law, at the beginning of the seventh year he had to allow the servant to take his freedom (Exodus 21:1-6).

Those hired servants would have performed their duties down to the finest detail. Even before the master got out of bed, his favourite slippers would be there for his feet. When he sat down to breakfast his favourite food would be ready for him to eat. Before the day dawned the servant would have been up and working. Are we in that place with God – are we ready to respond to whatever He desires?

The law of the day stated that the contract of the hired servant expired when the six years were up. Let me explain the setting...

Family members and other hired servants are all waiting to say their goodbyes to the servant before he leaves. The hired servant has given the other hired servants and their children one last hug.

But on seeing the master of the house waiting, the servant in his heart realises that his freedom will not be found in leaving the master's house – the freedom that really matters can be his through a simple choice!

Instead of bidding the Master farewell, he approaches the door post of the master's house and calls out to his master, "Pierce my ear, O lord!" (Exodus 21:6) He has decided not to go out free but to remain; he loves his master this much!

Once the master pierces the servant's ear, he is no longer the hired servant he was, employed for general duties. No, the true heart of the servant is now revealed. He is now in the house because of his love for the master. The master embraces him and welcomes him into the family, saying, "You are no longer a servant but a friend!" A friend may be defined as "one who is attached due to feelings."

In the story of the prodigal son, the self-righteous son who stayed at home had done his chores with the attitude of a servant. He did not understand that being his father's son meant being his friend as well. Voicing his envy, he said, "You are not part of us, you are not worthy, you are lesser than me – the fatted calf should not have been killed for you!"

Be careful not to go where pride seeks to take you, because pride will take you to a place where grace cannot keep you.

Don't be dismayed if people turn their backs on you, especially those who attend church meetings. Note that I didn't say "the church" – there's a difference!

What do you expect when you attend church? I expect God to be in the house, and that when He is there miracles will happen! But if God is not in the house, we might just as well be in a community gathering, singing choruses and raising our hands just for our own enjoyment. How far have we fallen?

28 *"...therefore came his father out, and entreated him.*

[29]*And he answering said to his father, Lo, these many years do I serve thee, neither transgressed I at any time thy commandment: and yet thou never gavest me a kid, that I might make merry with my friends:*

[30]*But as soon as this thy son was come, which hath devoured thy living with harlots, thou hast killed for him the fatted calf.*

[31]*And he said unto him, Son, thou art ever with me, and all that I have is thine.*

[32]*It was meet that we should make merry, and be glad: for this thy brother was dead, and is alive again; and was lost, and is found."*

God in His mercy reaches out even to the last moment. Judas Iscariot, who betrayed Jesus, sat at the Master's table almost to the end, yet still chose to go his own way. Friend, never choose your own way! There are but two ways in this life and one leads to life and the other leads to death. We are not our own, we have been bought with a price. The choice is clear – either follow God or follow the way that leads to destruction.

In Matthew, chapter 19, we read the story of the rich man…

[16]*"And, behold, one came and said unto him, Good Master, what good thing shall I do, that I may have eternal life?*

[17]*And he said unto him, Why callest thou me good? There is none good but one, that is, God: but if thou wilt enter into life, keep the commandments.*

[18]*He saith unto him, which? Jesus said, Thou shalt do no murder, Thou shalt not commit adultery, Thou shalt not steal, Thou shalt not bear false witness,*

[19]*Honour thy father and thy mother: and, Thou shalt love thy neighbour as thyself.*

[20]*The young man saith unto him, <u>all these things have I kept from my youth up: what lack I yet</u>?*

[21]*Jesus said unto him, if thou wilt be perfect, go and sell that thou hast, and give to the poor, and thou shalt have treasure in heaven: and come and follow me.*

[22]*But when the young man heard that saying, he went away sorrowful: for he had great possessions.*

[23]Then said Jesus unto his disciples, Verily I say unto you, that a rich man shall hardly enter into the kingdom of heaven.

[24]And again I say unto you, it is easier for a camel to go through the eye of a needle, than for a rich man to enter into the kingdom of God.

[25]When his disciples heard it, they were exceedingly amazed, saying, who then can be saved?

[26]But Jesus beheld them, and said unto them, with men this is impossible; but with God all things are possible.

This man, like the prodigal son's elder brother, kept the rules. But in both cases their hearts were not right. There was no compassion, no love, no relationship.

Jesus NEVER said that a rich man will never get into heaven! He said that it would be difficult for a rich man to get into heaven – not because he has riches but because the riches have him. Jesus, through "the word of knowledge" told this rich man – "Give it away!" But the rich man, who obeyed the letter of the Law, refused to obey the Spirit of the Law. The letter kills but the Spirit brings Life! This man was not just told the truth, the Truth was standing right in front of him, the Truth was speaking to him. Yet of his own will he turned away. Could it be that the Church is full of similar people, people who obey the letter but not the Spirit?

If you have been in what are called "the Faith churches", most likely you will have heard Matthew 19:26 many times and even know it by heart…but let's read it again.

"*…with God all things are possible.*"

We quote these words in prayer as though they were bullets in a machine gun – "With God all things are possible, with God all things are possible, with God all things are possible, with God..."

Have you ever realised that at its root this verse is not about the things of this world but about a will that's fully surrendered to the Father?

We can give God our tithes, offerings, singing, churchgoing time, prayer time, ministry time -- but if we not have given Him our will we have missed the verse's meaning.

When we surrender our will to Him, that "small voice" becomes more like a whisper, because His sheep know His voice. He does not need to shout for we are listening and are ready and willing to obey.

For those who live a surrendered will, Jesus is not on the outside trying to get in, but rather is on the inside revealing Himself out from us!

The greatest thing those who are like the rich man or the prodigal son could ever give to the Lord is their will. This includes you and me as well. Listen carefully: as long as we live on this earth we will never be totally dead to "self"! If that were so, Paul would never have written, "I die daily." If you are totally dead – guess what? You are dead! Self is a beast that will breathe alongside your spiritual man. Every day of our lives we live with the fact that the beast of self is trying to raise its ugly head, and every day those of us who live a surrendered life overcome it by choosing what the Spirit desires instead of what our flesh wants.

When the disciples asked how difficult would it be to enter into heaven, Jesus said, "...With God all things are possible." The key is "with God"! Get it deep within you – "with God"! He is the only One that can lead you to the altar of sacrifice where you place your will on the altar. Your flesh will cry out: "Please don't leave me here, for I am going to die!" It will remind you of the good times you had when you did your own will. It will call it good but for you to enter into that place that God has for you, no matter what, you need to place your will on the altar. God requires nothing less of you than a surrendered will. Lay your will before Him now. Lay it down and say those precious words that bring all Heaven to a standstill: "Not my will but Thy will be done."

Chapter 27

Where's My Crown?

In Northern Ireland, the country of my birth, we have an image of the Queen of England on our money and this declares that because she owns our money she owns our government. In other words, we are Subjects of the Crown.

In the days of the sword, countries were ruled by kings and queens, and what they said was done! Their authority was such that if you owned land and the King or the Queen wanted it – they got it! That was because under the rule of royalty wherever a King or Queen placed their feet the land became theirs. This is why countries have one authority over them and not two. The Bible tells us the reason why: *"...Every kingdom divided against itself is brought to desolation..."* (Luke 11:17)

When the Queen, the Monarch of our country, is about to visit one of our cities or towns, you can't help but notice the activity! People are out cleaning more than usual, the police are everywhere, children are handed flags to wave, and everyone who is going to see Her Majesty puts on their best clothes! Why? The Queen is coming!

When Royalty arrives, everyone notices. Police officers straighten and salute and soldiers stand to attention! Why? Someone who is higher in power has crossed their path.

Are you aware that God Himself has made you a king? Yes, you are a king!

Revelation 1:6 says, *"And hath made us kings and priests unto God and his Father; to him be glory and dominion forever and ever. Amen"*

Now, you might say, "I not so sure about that!" But notice that the Scripture says, "Hath made us kings...!" "Hath" is past tense. When the young shepherd David was out in the field caring for his sheep he had not read the memo from Heaven that was passed to the prophet Samuel. It told Samuel that God had already chosen one of Jesse's sons to be the King of Israel. (At the time Samuel didn't know which one, but God did!)

You and I are made kings when through the New Birth we come from the lineage of royalty through the Holy Spirit. When you were "born again" of the Holy Spirit, you joined the royal line of King Jesus. You are not just anybody, you are somebody! In God's sight you are a king. Revelation 19:16 confirms this: "On his (Jesus') robe and on his (Jesus') thigh he has this name written: "King of kings and Lord of lords."

Jesus is the "King of kings" and we as kings (small 'k') are under the KING! Have you come to terms with this yet? You are a king!

Years ago, when the teaching of 'Kingship' came through the body of Christ here in Ireland, it was taught that we are made kings in God to rule over people, because that is what a natural king does. Learning of this, many sought to enter ministry not to serve the Body of Christ but to rule over God's people. This was a wrong concept of kingship because we are called to serve one another. *"But he that is greatest among you shall be your servant." (*Matthew 23:11)

In their hearts the Master's disciples sought to be noticed, and quarrelled with another. Which of them was the greatest? Who should have the best seat in heaven? Then King Jesus with a towel and a basin of water took on himself the position of the lowest of all servants in any family, by kneeling down and washing His disciples' feet. Other than messing with the disciples minds really badly at this point what else was Jesus doing? The King was revealing Himself as a Servant!

When the Master took up that towel and basin He was demonstrating that although a King, He was also a servant, and as such his job was to ease the lives of others. Spiritually speaking, as we take up the servant's towel and basin we will see opportunities every day for us to minister to others. Please don't be like that priest or that Levite who could have helped the wounded man on the road but who, when they saw that he was bleeding crossed to the other side (Luke 10: 30-37). The trappings of their outer robes were more important to them than the inner robe of a servant, which is what God has called us to be. None of us should ever be so great in our own eyes that we believe that we can do without others. That priest and that Levite thought they could do without the man who had been attacked. But a Samaritan was willing to take up a towel and a basin and ease, as much as he could, the pain of hurt of that helpless, wounded man. Jesus said, "Go and do likewise!"

Are you willing to wash another's feet, even the feet of your partner? If God leads, are you willing to lay down your 'robes' of judgement and of recognition? Jesus wore the garment of a servant. Are you willing to lay aside your own will and put someone else ahead of you? Are you willing to lay aside that which so easily besets you for the prize that's waiting for you at the end of the race?

No matter who has done you wrong (and believe me when I say that as long as you live on this earth there will always be those who will do you wrong), are you willing to lift that basin and towel and with a loving heart wash the very feet of those who have rejected you?

Jesus said, *"If I then, your Lord and Master, have washed your feet, ye ought to wash one and another's feet. For I have given you an example, so that you should do as I have done unto you."* John 13:14, 15

An attitude of serving the Master by one another will enable us to keep everything in perspective, and will prevent us from falling into adultery for a title, a false dream or any other temptation. As we come to understand being a servant to each other it will release us from competing against each other, and will set us free to rule. And to rule what if not people? (1 Corinthians 12:21-27)

We all know that every King has a domain, a land over which he rules. But if we have been made kings, over what do we rule and where is our domain? The King of Jordan rules over Jordan and the King of Sweden rules over Sweden, so then the obvious question is: Who or what do you rule over?

The answer is YOU! Yes, that's right! You have been given dominion over you!

When you realise what I am saying you will see the folly of allowing pride to rule your life. Are you aware that our earthy origin means that we are pieces of land?

Genesis 3:19 says, *"...till thou return unto the ground; for out of it wast thou taken: for dust thou art, and unto dust shalt thou return."*

Adam was taken out of the ground, and since we are all Adam's descendants, we too have been taken from the ground! We are bio-degradable!

Yes, we may look at ourselves in mirrors and think of ourselves as being this or that, but you and I are nothing more than glorified pieces of land. (I am sure you are a nice piece of land.)

The Apostle Paul revealed this in 1 Corinthians 9:27, *"But I keep under my body, and bring it into subjection"*

Paul's 'land' was his body and Scripture tells us that he brought his land into a place of subjection, in other words his land became a subject of King Paul who served under the much greater King Jesus.

God made you king of your own body, which is your land, and you are to rule your own body. Each time you feel that flesh rising, kneel before the One who is greater than you, the King of Kings. When we as kings kneel to the higher authority of the King of kings, everything under the King also kneels. All temptation must then bow before you, because everyone and everything must be lower than the King!

Romans 12:1

"I beseech you therefore, brethren, (Any Christian) by the mercies of God, that ye present your bodies a living sacrifice, holy, acceptable unto God, which is your reasonable service.

As you bring your thinking into line with being a king you may just need to straighten that crown on your head. As Lamentations 5:16 says, *"The crown is fallen from our head: woe unto us that we have sinned!"*

When we become servants of one another and rule as kings over our own lives, our crowns will sit more firmly in place on our heads, and that which has been squatting on our land will then have to go -- in Jesus' Name!

It's time for us to humble ourselves as servants, so that we can live as kings unto God under an open heaven!

Chapter 28

Changing Eternity

The plane was being made ready to leave London's Heathrow airport. A brother in the Lord and I had been sitting together for several hours waiting for our connecting flight to India as we were going there to minister at several leaders' conferences. As we sat there, perspiration began to pour out of me and my stomach began to turn like a washing machine on spin. My body was wracked with sickness when it was announced over the intercom: "We will be boarding the plane in ten minutes!"

Ahead of me was a ten hour journey on the airplane, and feeling the way that I now did, I knew that it was unlikely that I would make it to my destination.

As I continue to share this story, keep in mind the theme of the previous chapter: that God has made each one of us a king over our own land, that is, over our body.

I said to the brother in the Lord, "Look after my bags, I'm off to the bathroom!" I remember going through the door into the bathroom and feeling this holy anger rise from within me, and before I knew what was happening, this authority came from within me, commanding out loud, "In the Name of Jesus, I take authority over this sickness, and out you must go from every part of me!" I really felt weak as I repeated the statement, "In the Name of Jesus I take authority over this sickness and out you must go from every part of me!" I walked over to the mirrors and looked directly into them and said, "One of us is leaving this room and it's not you devil, you are staying right here!" I turned around and it was only when I was walking out the doors that I thought, I never checked to see if anyone else was in the cubicles! Without the slightest exaggeration, I tell you that when I walked out of that bathroom I felt that I had a brand new body, there was no sickness in any part of me! What had happened?

An enemy agent had tried to set up camp on my land but the authority of a king had risen within me and driven it out!

The devil had tried to come against my ministry trip to India, but had forgotten that the crown I wore as a king enabled me to exercise regal authority.

You may feel that you are not worth it. You may have fallen into sin and gotten out of God's will. But as I said before, we've all 'missed it' at some point or we would not have needed the perfect Lamb of God. The reason Jesus came was because no man on this earth could ever walk without falling – our trust needed to be in Christ alone.

It is important for you to know that what God has begun in you He is well able to finish. Otherwise He would not have begun it! (Luke 14:28)

Have you ever taken the time to think about how important you are to God? You're so important to Him that He sent His only Son into this world so that you could be forgiven and walk as an overcomer on this earth.

I could say that you are so important to God that He allowed you to come to the point of time where the eyes of your understanding could be opened!

But what I really want to bring you is the question that God asked me. I have not shared this very often but I will share it with you.

Forget about all the people who have accused you, spoken badly of you or never spoken to you at all. This was the same boat Jesus was in, so who better to be there with you! Yes, we have all been in this boat – it's the 'elder brother syndrome' that we looked at earlier. But you must rise above it, and now here's how God caused me to do that.

What I like about God is that when He speaks or comes to you in some way He creates what I call, "The fingerprint of God on your life." There I was, minding my own business, working away in a timber yard by myself -- or so I thought. At the time I was singing a worship song to God in my heart.

Then it happened! Out of nowhere God spoke to me with a statement that impacted me so much that I actually had to grasp hold of the work bench. He said, "Are you ready? *Will you change eternity?*"

I had never heard anything like this before in my life. *"Will you change eternity?"*

My mind was now taking a bad beating, as we would say. You see, I knew that it was God who was speaking, but somehow or other my mind had gone into search mode in the way that a computer does. How could this be? Who can change eternity? I am only me. No, I can't do it -- it was Jesus who did that!

Then the question came again, and I want you too to take it on board: *"Will you change eternity?"*

Then, before I could get the 'ifs', buts' and 'whys' out, God asked me another question, one that I will now pass on to you. He said, *"Are you My son?"* Or if you are His daughter, I am sure that He would let me change it to, "Are you My daughter?" I answered, "Yes, I am Your son!" He then asked, *"Was Jesus My Son?"* That drove home to me that we are sons and daughters of God, and that what Jesus is we are as well! I replied with tears in my eyes, "Yes!" Then He said, *"My Son changed eternity, now will you?"* I said, "Yes!"

Eternity is there to be changed - if Jesus as the Son of God could change eternity, then you and I as God's sons and daughters can also change eternity. You might think this very deep, but listen my friend, when I say that the fight for your life is not just about you; it is also about eternity, which is a very long time!

I am sure that many things went through your mind when I asked you that question, just as they did when God asked it of me. This is because of its depth and because of responsibility that's implicit in it. I can share a number of stories about eternity being changed, but let me share one in which a woman decided to change eternity, and guess what? It's in the Bible!

John 2

1 *"And the third day there was a marriage in Cana of Galilee; and the mother of Jesus was there:*

2 *And both Jesus was called, and his disciples, to the marriage.*

3 *And when they wanted wine, the mother of Jesus saith unto him, They have no wine.*

[4]Jesus saith unto her, Woman, what have I to do with thee? Mine hour is not yet come.

[5]His mother saith unto the servants, whatsoever he saith unto you, do it.

[6]And there were set there six water pots of stone, after the manner of the purifying of the Jews, containing two or three firkins apiece.

[7]Jesus saith unto them, Fill the water pots with water. And they filled them up to the brim.

[8]And he saith unto them, Draw out now, and bear unto the governor of the feast. And they bare it.

[9]When the ruler of the feast had tasted the water that was made wine, and knew not whence it was: (but the servants who drew the water knew) the governor of the feast called the bridegroom,

[10]And saith unto him, every man at the beginning doth set forth good wine; and when men have well drunk, then that which is worse: but thou hast kept the good wine until now.

[11]This beginning of miracles did Jesus in Cana of Galilee, and manifested forth his glory; and his disciples believed on him."

Can you see how eternity was changed in this story? Mary the mother of Jesus is invited to a marriage celebration, and so Jesus and His disciples go with her. Until now Jesus has done no miracles (v 4) but Mary sees into eternity and sees that her son is more than her son, that He is the Son of God. Time protests, No, it's not for today! (v4) But Mary steps beyond 'Not' into 'Why Not' and in so doing brings a miracle out of the future and into the present.

Because Mary dares to pull eternity into time, Jesus brings forward a miracle from tomorrow into today! He does it because His mother Mary asks Him to! Did God ask Mary, "Will you change eternity?" Who knows? But one thing I do know and I hope you see it, is that what was destined for the future has now been brought forward into the present! Why? Simply because Mary believed that eternity could be changed.

You may have been listening as "old claw nails" (the devil) told you that you will never be close to God again, that you have come too far down the road you are on, that what you've just read will not work for you. If so, you must realise that in yourself of course you cannot do it. We are all under a master, whether it be God or the devil. We are all walking one of two paths in this life – God's path or the devil's path - for no one can serve two masters. (Matt. 6:24) Whose path do you wish to be on?

To live outside 'the chicken factory' and be detached from the system will bring you unto the path of abundant Life where God becomes real and your life is never the same again. For this to happen there must be a surrendering to God which will lead to a hunger for Him. When that hunger erupts from your spirit the mysteries of God will be drawn unto you, bringing life to your spirit.

God's mysteries are not found in knowledge but in revelation. But to obtain the mysteries one must sacrifice all that is between you and God. Every adulterous item must be smashed in your thinking for He will not allow any other gods to stand in front of Him before He gives you the manna (Revelation) of heaven.

Do you know all revelation is layered? Let's go to Scripture…

Matthew 16:13

"When Jesus came into the coasts of Caesarea Philippi, he asked his disciples, saying, Whom do men say that I the Son of man am?

14 And they said, Some say that thou art John the Baptist: some, Elias; and others, Jeremias, or one of the prophets.

15 He saith unto them, But whom say ye that I am?

16 And Simon Peter answered and said, Thou art the Christ, the Son of the living God.

17 And Jesus answered and said unto him, Blessed art thou, Simon Barjona: for flesh and blood hath not revealed it unto thee, but my Father which is in heaven.

18 And I say also unto thee, That thou art Peter, and upon this rock I will build my church; and the gates of hell shall not prevail against it.

19 And I will give unto thee the keys of the kingdom of heaven: and whatsoever thou shalt bind on earth shall be bound in heaven: and whatsoever thou shalt loose on earth shall be loosed in heaven."

Jesus asks the guys who have hung out with him for approximately three years, His disciples, "Whom do men say that I the Son of man am?"

They respond by what they have heard, (knowledge) "You are John the Baptist, Elias (Elijah), Jeremias (Jeremiah) or another prophet. "

But notice the question – Whom do men say I am? Jesus did not ask "who does God say I am?" for HE knew He was 'sent' (one with a mission) from God, but "who do men say I am?" They respond with the names of dead people but then Peter steps up to the mark, when he steps from knowledge (what he heard) into revelation (what is revealed) and said, "Thou art Christ the Son of the Living God." And Jesus responds, "…flesh and blood (man) hath not revealed this unto thee, but my Father in heaven."

What happened? Peter reached from time (that which he knows) into eternity (that which God knows) and brought eternity into time declaring "thou are Christ..." Now do you see the significance in what Jesus meant? "Only My Father could reveal this to you! Peter had to step into God to reveal God! Hallelujah! Jesus follows on by saying, "And I say also unto thee, that thou art Peter and upon this rock I will build my church."

What was the rock? Revelation! It is revelation that gives insight and therefore empowers us to walk all over this Adulterous Spirit and to stay free from the system. For the devil knows the gates of hell cannot prevail from that which is eternal – revelation.

Knowledge is an earthly currency while heavens currency is revelation unending – why? Because that which comes from God never ends!

I challenge you as the whistle of the Holy Spirit blows to begin the last part of your life! Under God this can be the very best part, the most fulfilling part, the most rewarding part, the most anointed part! Hear the whistle blowing and see the angels lining up in the stands beating their wings in adoration! Not for you and me but for the King who yet again has caused His Holy Spirit to bring about resurrection – this time in you! Remove all deception, lies and cheating! Cut off any immoral affairs of the heart and renew your vows to the King of kings and to your legal partner in life. When you do you'll be ready to take to the field of life with renewed spiritual vigour! You can start afresh, but only after a fresh cleansing from the Blood of the Lamb. See God's hand that opened up the Red Sea open over your life, God's voice calling you to a new dream, a new purpose in Him, and for each other if you are married. Take that step closer to the One who is forever for you! Can I ask you again the question that God asked me? *"Will you change eternity?"* Stand up and be counted. Say "Yes!" Don't let another day go by without yielding your life to the Master.

Changing eternity takes place a step at a time, when you take one step away from deception and one step closer to the truth. Remember eternity does not start when we die, eternity starts when His Holy Spirit (Eternal God) comes and dwells within. Take the step that I did and God will bless you more than you could ever imagine!

Set aside the Third Party of adultery, and cling entirely to God. He who has begun a good work in you will perform it until as "A Bride Prepared" you will be ready for the Groom when He returns.

Let's pray.

"Father, we come before you right now in the power of the Holy Spirit. We acknowledge that there is no one like "You", and so we are deeply honoured that we can come now into your throne room through prayer. I lift before you my new found friend, the one who has been deeply troubled in the past, and I ask right now that you come in your love and surround this one with your presence. Help him or her to know that there is a God in Heaven that has revealed Himself on this earth in the person of His Son! Now Lord, we lift before you the path this one is on, and we ask that if it is not leading in the direction that You desire, that your Spirit would bear witness to the path for this one You have prepared.

We ask for a fresh cleansing of the Blood of Jesus over this life, that the spirit would be cleansed from abuse, the soul energized with a desire to live out in the open, and that no form of deception will ever take root again. We take the axe of the Word and cut off from every life the roots of deception, fear, addiction, fear of loss, rejection, lack of identity due to adoption, and the fear of never being loved. We release them from any form of mental abuse, images, torment, abuse, ignorance and sexual activities outside of marriage. We ask that the thoughts they have will line up with *Your* thoughts, and that the life and the health of each one would take a new direction as they turn to *You.*

We also submit to you, Lord, the iniquities of our forefathers. We repent of our lack of forgiveness and of any form of bitterness. Let each one say to *You*, "O God, cleanse me from all sin and iniquity, I place the

Blood of Jesus on the door posts of my mind. I am what *You* say I am! I forgive those who have wronged me. I hold no one responsible for what I have done or for what I have become. I am now totally committed to the truth that from this moment on, my life, old and new, is hid in Christ; that my sins have been washed away; that the iniquities of my forefathers has no right to seek payment against me. I will praise *You*, for I am fearfully and wonderfully made! Marvellous are *Your* works, and that my soul well knows.

"Thank you for bringing Truth into my life. Thank you for setting me free. Thank you that my life can now only get better." I say "God, bring it on! Bring it on God Style, and let me see the glory that was hidden from me." I love *You*, my Father, my Redeemer, and my Saviour. Thank you for setting me FREE!

If you have prayed this prayer/ this book has revealed His path to you I would love to hear from you.

Inspired to write a book?

Contact

www.ingramcontent.com/pod-product-compliance
Ingram Content Group UK Ltd.
Pitfield, Milton Keynes, MK11 3LW, UK
UKHW020141250726
13967UKWH00002B/791